# Steering Clear

# Steering Clear

How to Avoid a Debt Crisis
and Secure Our Economic Future

## Peter G. Peterson

PORTFOLIO / PENGUIN

PORTFOLIO / PENGUIN

Published by the Penguin Group
Penguin Group (USA) LLC
375 Hudson Street
New York, New York 10014

USA | Canada | UK | Ireland | Australia | New Zealand | India | South Africa | China
penguin.com
A Penguin Random House Company

First published by Portfolio / Penguin, a member of
Penguin Group (USA) LLC, 2015

ISBN 978-1-59184-780-9

Printed in the United States of America
1  3  5  7  9  10  8  6  4  2

Set in ITC New Baskerville Std
Designed by Neuwirth & Associates, Inc.

*This book is dedicated to my grandchildren Alexandra, Beau, Chloe, Drew, Eliza, Jack, Peter Cary, Steven, and Xander, and to all young people. This next generation of Americans has the most to gain, and has the most at stake, in how we build our fiscal and economic future.*

# PREFACE

For more than twenty-five years, I have been writing and thinking about a confluence of forces that threatens America's long-term economic future, including our rapidly aging society, our growing healthcare costs, our vast unfunded entitlement programs, our flawed tax system, and our dysfunctional political system with its myopic inability to compromise or reconcile rigid ideologies. This combination of factors leaves us with the sobering prospect of massive, unsustainable long-term debt that I consider a transcendent threat to future generations.

Yet in spite of repeated short-term fiscal squabbles, including debt limits, sequesters, and government shutdowns, this long-term debt threat remains unaddressed. The drama-filled, economically damaging budget battles of the last few years have focused almost entirely on the near term—putting aside the more difficult, but much more important, long-term questions.

Several years ago, I retired from business and considered what I might do that would be both fulfilling and meaningful. It seemed obvious to me that our nation's unsustainable, long-term structural fiscal challenges would be a worthy subject and I established a foundation to draw attention to—and make progress on—that issue.

Creatively titled the Peter G. Peterson Foundation, this organization would create more awareness of the long-term debt problem, its size, its causes, and its effects. The foundation would also discuss general principles for reform as well as policy proposals themselves. The foundation would be nonpartisan and would not endorse any particular reform proposal. Rather, we would work to educate, engage, and convene a variety of perspectives on this issue.

A good example of this approach was our 2011–12 Solutions Initiative project. We went to six think tanks from across the ideological and political spectrum, from left to right. To start with, did they agree or disagree that the long-term debt balloon was unsustainable? All six agreed. Did they have their favorite proposal? They all said yes (though they all had different proposals). We then asked if they would be willing to lay out their plan for achieving a sustainable debt level within twenty-five years, and they agreed. We then highlighted the groups' findings at our annual Fiscal Summit in Washington, D.C., and distributed their ideas widely, demonstrating that there were many viable paths forward for policymakers.

Now, while it's clear that options are available, it's also unmistakable that there are very strongly held—and sometimes incompatible—philosophical views on either side. One view, held by many conservatives, is that we should solve our fiscal challenges with spending cuts alone. The view from the opposite side of the political spectrum holds that cuts to entitlement programs should be off limits, in favor of imposing higher taxes, particularly on the rich. Both approaches are not only extreme in their impact, but they are also politically infeasible.

Putting aside one's ideology, it's clear that for any plan to be politically viable for the long term, it must have bipartisan support. Therefore, any durable set of long-term reforms must combine both spending cuts and revenue increases. I further believe that both the revenue and spending reforms should have the heaviest impact on the well off—like me!

Given all this prologue, what am I attempting to do (and not do) with this book? One of the key concepts that I hope to get across in this book is the importance of thinking longer term. As a nation, we are all too focused on this year, or next, and often ignore and delay important decisions that affect the next generation. While many of my critics have labeled me a deficit scold (or worse) who is singularly obsessed with cutting entitlements and immediate austerity, the truth is that I am not principally concerned with this year's deficit, or next year's or even those over the next ten years. Nor do I favor fiscal austerity in this time of unusual economic distress. And I resolutely believe that we must reform vitally important entitlement programs in a way that retains and strengthens their value for our most vulnerable citizens—particularly as we've seen trou-

bling trends in wage stagnation and disturbing facts about income immobility in recent decades. Rather, my primary
concern is the longer term unsustainable path of our debt and
the threat that it poses to the American dream.

Lastly, I should explain that this book reflects my personal
views, not those of the foundation itself or its staff.

I hope you find this book informative, and that it adds to
this critically important conversation about America's future.

# CONTENTS

# Steering Clear

# INTRODUCTION

O n a clear, moonless April night in 1912, wireless operators
aboard the RMS *Titanic*—en route to New York on its
maiden voyage—received a series of messages from other
ships warning of large icebergs in the area through which it
was to pass. The captain, despite knowing that icebergs would
be hard to spot on a moonless night on a flat sea, did not post
extra lookouts or slow down. Instead, given his confidence in
his mighty ocean liner, he ordered his crew to maintain a high
cruising speed, and after a fine supper with prominent passengers, retired to his cabin. At 11:40 p.m., the *Titanic*'s look-
out spotted an iceberg looming ahead and raised the alarm.

Despite an immediate hard turn and engines at full reverse,
the *Titanic*'s momentum toward the massive berg was too great
to avoid a collision. And as the implacable ice gashed open the

ship's heavy steel hull, water began gushing in. The captain, realizing the peril of the situation, sent out a distress signal and ordered an evacuation of the ship. But the ship was not built with enough lifeboats for everyone on board because the ship owners were so confident that their ship would never sink. And the captain and crew were just as unprepared: lifeboat drills were never conducted, passengers were not assigned specific boats, and the deck officers did not know how to properly load them. Because of an appalling lack of planning and preparation, many of the lifeboats were launched only half full. Just two hours and forty minutes after the collision, as the doomed ship's orchestra played bravely to the last, the "unsinkable" *Titanic* suddenly reached a tipping point and plunged into eternity.

The *Titanic*'s sinking was a tragedy—and not just because 1,500 people lost their lives. It was a tragedy because its deadly collision was entirely avoidable. In haste and hubris, the captain and his officers had ignored many clear warnings, dismissed the potential for danger, and refused to exercise even modest caution. Given such flawed decision making, it's clear that what ultimately caused the *Titanic*'s sinking was not so much a failure of the ship's design, but of leadership. And as such, the famous disaster should serve as a stark warning to all those who refuse to acknowledge and prepare for known dangers—of any sort—that lie over the horizon.

Unfortunately, despite clear danger and explicit warnings, the United States of America—distracted by short-term challenges and its own political dysfunction—is steaming toward its own collision, one with long-term debt.

# JUST HOW BIG COULD AMERICA'S LONG-TERM DEBT BECOME?

I'm not talking about current deficits, or the $13 trillion in public debt we've already amassed.* Given the size of our economy, it's still manageable. What I am focused on is the danger and unsustainability of our long-term debt. That's because the math over the next twenty-five years is clear: if we fail to

## U.S. DEBT HELD BY THE PUBLIC IS ON AN UNSUSTAINABLE PATH

**Debt Held by the Public** (Percentage of GDP)

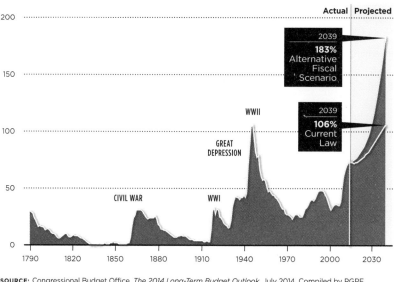

SOURCE: Congressional Budget Office, *The 2014 Long-Term Budget Outlook,* July 2014. Compiled by PGPF.
NOTE: Data for the alternative fiscal scenario includes economic feedback.

*These numbers reflect debt held by the public. Gross debt (which also includes intragovernmental debt held by the trust funds) is $18 trillion.

address the growing gap between projected spending and revenues, the Congressional Budget Office (CBO) projects, under what I consider to be optimistic so-called current-law assumptions, that our federal debt will grow to 106 percent of the size of our entire national economy. Under less optimistic assumptions, our debt could soar to an unsustainable 183 percent of gross domestic product (GDP) within twenty-five years.

To put that level of debt into some perspective, 183 percent would far exceed the highest in our nation's history. As a percentage of GDP—which enables an apples-to-apples comparison over time—it would be nearly *double* that which we incurred in the 1940s, when we were fighting World War II.

## WHY I AM SPEAKING OUT

Now, some people might wonder why I am so persistent in sounding the alarm over America's long-term debt. After all, why should an eighty-eight-year-old billionaire—by any measure long on dollars and short on years—care so deeply about an issue that to many people seems both distant and arcane?

The answer is simple: I am an American Dreamer, and this country has given my family and me—and millions of others—unequaled opportunities to dream and to prosper. And together we have a profound obligation to try to pass on the same opportunity to future generations. This isn't just an economic imperative; it's a moral imperative. The quintessentially American opportunity to work hard and achieve one's highest aspirations—once available to nearly everyone—has begun to sputter. And unless we can reignite this opportunity and get "back in the future business," as President Bill Clinton puts it, the American middle class—whose continued growth, optimism, and spirit of possibility lie at the core of our nation's prosperity—will founder. And if the middle class founders, eventually our democracy may too.

If we fail to get our long-term debt under control, we will likely confront one or perhaps two very different economic challenges—either one of which would produce profoundly negative consequences for our nation and its future.


## THE PERILS OF A MARKET CRISIS

The first risk is that of a sovereign debt crisis brought about by a sudden loss of market confidence in U.S. debt. Cumulatively, a continuation of shenanigans like the 2013 fiscal cliff, debt-ceiling showdowns, and sequesters that harm economic growth without meaningfully addressing our long-term debt could at some point undermine our government's credibility at home and abroad. If that happened, a seemingly small event might trigger an avalanche of consequences—not just harming economic growth, but potentially unraveling the social safety net for the most vulnerable Americans. While interest rates remain low and such a crisis may seem remote today, no one knows when a market-driven crisis might hit, or how bad it could be. And as ugly as fiscal politics may seem today, they will only become uglier in a time of severe crisis—precisely when we would need cooperation and bipartisanship most.

The lengthy crisis in Europe, which very few predicted, is a good example of what can happen when markets suddenly turn. Before the crisis, most European governments could easily borrow money at low rates. But there were serious underlying challenges—especially in Greece—that policymakers let fester. And then the markets turned. Greece defaulted, and other European governments—many experiencing soaring interest rates and sinking credit ratings—struggled to avoid a similar fate. In late 2009, Greek interest rates on ten-year government debt hovered between 4.5 and 5.5 percent. By early 2011, that rate had soared to 12 percent—and by early 2012, it was climbing past 25 percent. The attendant economic problems that have subsequently afflicted much of the Continent—with persistently low growth and persistently high unemployment, especially among young people who face unemployment rates above 55 percent in Greece—have made it even harder for Europe to take the steps necessary to put its fiscal house in order.

To be clear, the United States isn't very likely to find itself in the same situation as Greece. But the larger point remains true: the underlying conditions of market crises don't necessarily develop overnight. Rather, they build over time as leaders chase short-term political gains at the cost of their nation's long-term fiscal health. Ultimately, markets for government debt can turn quickly and unexpectedly, often with disastrous consequences. And while such a crisis could belatedly force leaders to address long-term debt, it would also drive up the costs of doing so—far more so than if our leaders were to tackle the long-term debt steadily, over time.

## THE PERILS OF A
## SLOW-GROWTH ECONOMY

The second type of economic threat we could face, and one that many economists consider more likely, is that our mounting long-term debt could cause an extended period of slow growth. In such a slow-growth economy, rising deficits and increasing federal interest payments would eventually crowd out the very sort of private and public investments necessary to compete and grow in an increasingly technological and knowledge-driven world.

Investing heavily in the future has always been an American strength. Building the interstate highways, exploring space, developing GPS technology, mapping the human genome—these were all possible because we had the political, intellectual, and financial resources to make major, long-term investments. If we spend too much of our national income on runaway healthcare costs and massive interest payments instead of investing in true catalysts for growth, the United States could eventually risk losing out to other countries in achieving the next great scientific and engineering breakthroughs. Indeed, there are some indicators suggesting that this may be happening already.

America's interest costs are already on a pace to march upward in coming years as the economy recovers and interest rates rise to traditional levels. In 2014, total federal interest costs were 1.3 percent of GDP. But by 2050, the CBO projects that interest costs could rise to a staggering 10.7 percent of GDP. At that level, interest expense would be *four times* what the federal government has historically spent each year on education and job training, R&D, and nondefense infrastructure *combined,* which are vitally needed for long-term growth. (See the chart on page 63.) And we will face these high interest costs at a time when investing in the future should be a national imperative.

In sum, the more we spend on our nation's interest payments, the less we will have to invest in our nation's future. And as anyone who has ever seen his or her personal finances devastated by credit card bills knows, interest payments have a voracious appetite for resources that could—and should—be invested in building a better future, not paying for the past. Yet the past, unfortunately, is what interest payments are largely about.

## WHAT ARE THE BIGGEST DRIVERS OF AMERICA'S LONG-TERM DEBT?

For many years now, I have been speaking and writing about the demographic and economic trends that threaten the economic dynamism that has enabled the United States to prosper like no other nation in history. At the heart of our long-term fiscal challenge is a simple failure to reconcile two sides of our federal budget: the programs and benefits we want our government to provide, and the revenue necessary to pay for them. Yet this is an incomplete picture. There are several complex and powerful trends that are widening the gap between spending and revenue, including high and rising healthcare costs, growing spending on retirement programs, and an inadequate tax system.

The biggest trend affecting long-term spending between now and 2040 is the retirement of the nearly eighty million men and women who make up the baby boom generation. The first wave of the baby boom generation turned sixty-five in 2011, and the last wave won't turn sixty-five until 2029. (See the chart on page 74.) Not surprisingly, the fiscal consequences of these big demographic changes won't begin to be really felt until the 2020s.

In coming decades, increasing life spans will also raise the amount of time that such people spend in retirement. Indeed, a man reaching age sixty-five today is expected to live 6.6 years longer than he was in 1940, shortly after Social Security was set up. For women, life expectancy at age sixty-five has increased 6.9 years. Combined with rising per-person costs for healthcare, these demographic changes will contribute to higher spending on programs such as Social Security, Medicare, and Medicaid, which are vital to older Americans.

In looking at the federal budget, keep in mind that the CBO does not project that all entitlement programs will contribute to long-term spending pressure. In fact, some entitlement programs—such as food assistance, unemployment compensation, and family and foster care—play virtually no role in driving long-term spending and will shrink as a share of the economy, according to the CBO.

Instead, spending pressure is coming from just a handful of entitlement programs. (See the chart on page 72.) Given the demographics, Social Security spending is projected to grow steadily. But the biggest increase in federal spending in coming decades will be associated with providing healthcare through Medicare (which subsidizes medical costs for people sixty-five and older), Medicaid (which subsidizes medical costs for low-income people of all ages), and federal subsidies for health insurance (purchased by lower-income people on the new healthcare exchanges created by the Affordable Care Act).

# SOARING HEALTHCARE COSTS ARE PROJECTED TO DRIVE UP ENTITLEMENT SPENDING

Currently, Americans spend more than twice as much on healthcare per person than citizens in other major countries do, and yet many of our health outcomes are no better—and some are actually worse. For example, our life expectancy is in the bottom third among advanced nations, and our infant mortality rate is one of the worst.

Our healthcare sector as a whole is plagued with systemic problems that both keep costs high and drive costs up at a pace much faster than mere inflation would otherwise cause. Among these are

- fee-for-service payments that perversely incentivize doctors to perform more procedures rather than focus on the outcome of patient health and that encourage the development and proliferation of cost-increasing medical technology;

- perverse tax incentives that subsidize employer-provided insurance and dull employees' awareness of its full cost;

- many new technologies in healthcare that actually drive costs up instead of down and often lead to little or no improvement in health outcomes;

- fragmented and unusable data about healthcare costs and outcomes;

- a lack of price transparency that makes it hard for patients to know the price of their treatments or to comparison shop;

- concern about lawsuits that causes physicians to practice expensive defensive medicine; and

- inefficient and excessive administrative costs.

Worse, this list is hardly exhaustive. Left unchecked, these and other factors are projected by the CBO to push private and public consumption of healthcare from 16 percent of

GDP today to 22 percent by 2039. That would represent nine times what the U.S. government and our private companies combined spend on R&D annually, on average.

Not only will many more older Americans be relying on these increasingly costly healthcare programs in coming decades, but many of them will be relying on them much longer than their counterparts in past generations. For example, although the number of people aged eighty-five years and older is still relatively small, it is projected to be the fastest-growing age segment in the population. Over the next twenty-five years, this age group will swell from six million to fourteen million people. Without a doubt, this development has significant budgetary effects, as the average health costs of people in this group are more than five times the average costs of those aged nineteen to sixty-four.

The rapid growth in U.S. healthcare costs has slowed somewhat in recent years, but it is unclear how much of this slowdown was caused by a weak economy and whether the improvement will last. The federal government's healthcare programs still face a challenging future in light of population aging. In coming decades, tens of millions of elderly Americans will become eligible for federal healthcare programs and despite revising its projections downward to reflect the recent slowdown in health costs, the CBO projects that within twenty-five years, federal health spending as a share of GDP will be double its level in 1999. (See the chart on page 94.) Although the Affordable Care Act ("Obamacare") introduced some cost-control measures, that legislation was primarily focused on reducing the number of uninsured, not on slowing the growth of costs. Regardless of growth trends, our current healthcare system is highly inefficient compared with other countries and this inefficiency should be addressed.

In my view, nothing could be more important to overcoming our nation's long-term debt challenge than figuring out how to deliver better care to more people at a cost we can actually afford. This is why the Peter G. Peterson Foundation, which I launched in 2008, is establishing a healthcare center whose primary mission is to drive improvements and achieve better healthcare outcomes at a lower cost. The center is aiming to identify the successful models that could—and should—be scaled up.

## SOCIAL SECURITY COSTS WILL ALSO DRIVE UP ENTITLEMENT SPENDING

A secondary driver of projected long-term spending is the mismatch between Social Security revenues and benefits. Social Security will be running increasingly large deficits in the future. (See the chart on page 81.)

Social Security is the nation's principal bulwark against poverty in old age. The program provides significant financial support to sixty million Americans, many of whom are economically vulnerable. (See the chart on page 79.)

If we don't soon address Social Security's long-term unsustainability, we risk harming those who rely on the program the most. As a nation, we cannot let this happen. That is why we need reforms to these programs that will protect the most vulnerable while asking the well off to make the largest sacrifices. This threat to the safety net isn't hypothetical. It's an actuarial reality, and it's why we need to have an honest conversation about which benefits are both necessary and affordable, and who is going to pay for them while still funding other critical priorities.

Moreover, the solutions for Social Security are well known, have been thoroughly analyzed, and are readily available. Yet nothing has been done because there has never been enough political support—or courage—to tackle this issue seriously. So year after year the Social Security problem remains unsolved.

## GETTING SERIOUS ABOUT GUNS AND BUTTER

A third important factor the United States must consider is military spending. Not so much because peacetime military spending is a big contributor to long-term debt, but because economic strength and military strength are ultimately inseparable. In my view, escalating long-term debt—much of which is often held by foreign lenders—can undermine our national security more than any far-off, belligerent dictator ever could. This viewpoint has been forthrightly articulated by Admiral Michael Mullen, former chairman of the Joint Chiefs of Staff. As he said in 2010, "The most significant threat to our national security is our debt."

Maintaining economic strength over long periods of time is absolutely vital, as the United States learned during the Cold War, which lasted a half century. Unfortunately, our armed forces are still geared, in many ways, to fight the last century's Cold War instead of this century's more diverse and distributed threats. According to the Stockholm International Peace Research Institute, the United States currently spends more on its military than the next eight countries *combined*. (See the chart on page 120.) Significant aspects of this spending are not driven by a modern, coherent defense strategy based on today's emerging threats, but by pork-barrel politics and yesterday's threats.

Times have changed. New global powers are emerging. Some old threats have slowly dissipated. New threats—many of which didn't exist before information technology became so integral and important to our infrastructure and economy—are ascendant. Meanwhile, our defense resources are no longer unlimited, and so we have to be smarter—a lot smarter—about every dollar we spend, and every dollar we don't. In short, we need a new defense strategy for a new era.

To help spark this overdue discussion, the Peterson Foundation made a grant to the Stimson Center to convene a panel of top national security experts—including retired military officers at the highest levels—to study how the United States should best address the evolving threats of today's world. This Defense Advisory Committee issued a comprehensive report detailing a strategy for how the United States can increasingly rely on unprecedented agility, technological superiority, as well as the global reach of its naval, space, and air forces.* The report recognizes newer national security needs, such as protecting critical civilian, government, and military infrastructure from cyber attack and countering the nuclear threat from belligerent nations and terrorists. At the same time, the committee proposes ways to safely and significantly reduce the size of our ground forces by up to one third. Under such a strategy, ground forces would be deployed into substantial combat far less frequently, and only with well-defined and limited objectives. Our nuclear forces could also be scaled back consistent with the changes in the world since the end of the Cold War.

In addition to maintaining a smarter, contemporary defense posture using more limited resources, we also need to address another aspect of defense spending: the cost of retirement benefits and healthcare for the U.S. military. Like Social Security, Medicare, and Medicaid, these costs also will add up quickly over the decades. We need to do a better job of reining in such costs in order to preserve resources while at the same time continuing to honor our commitments to our veterans.

Under Department of Defense secretaries Robert Gates, Leon Panetta, and Chuck Hagel, there have been efforts to reset military priorities. I was pleased to see a proposal from the Pentagon in early 2014 for a substantial reduction in

---

*Stimson Center, "A New U.S. Defense Strategy for a New Era: Military Superiority, Agility, and Efficiency" (Washington, D.C.: Stimson Center, November 2012), www.stimson.org/books-reports/a-new-us-defense-strategy-for-a-new-era-military-superiority-agility-and-efficiency/.

ground forces in coming years. However, too often, sensible reform proposals have met stiff opposition from special interests, and a considerable amount of work remains to be done to define and implement a new defense strategy and to ensure that budget allocations in this era of constrained resources are consistent with it.

## CONFRONTING AMERICA'S FISCAL REALITY BEFORE IT'S TOO LATE

Not surprisingly, a lot of people are uncomfortable confronting the monumental challenge of long-term debt. This includes many elected officials across the country, and thousands of lobbyists whose short-term, self-interested agendas often undermine long-term goals and responsibilities.

But for me, what's far more uncomfortable than confronting the challenge of our long-term debt is *not* confronting it. Because of my previous books on this topic and my advocacy in this arena, some people have labeled me a deficit scold. After all, I've been at this a long time: I cofounded the Bipartisan Budget Appeal of five hundred government, business, and academic leaders in 1982. A decade later, I cofounded the Concord Coalition with senators Warren Rudman and Paul Tsongas. Deficit reduction has been a major focus of my public life.

Given this earlier work, some critics dismiss me as a man who is obsessed with today's large deficits. Others accuse me of being in favor of immediate austerity. Neither is true. Ultimately, I am not principally concerned with this year's deficit, or next year's, or even those over the next ten years. As I emphasized earlier, my overwhelming focus is on our unsustainable *long-term* debt, which is not only the far more serious problem but one that is receiving far, far too little attention.

I do not favor fiscal austerity in this time of economic distress while our vulnerable economy is still in recovery. To the contrary, I believe that any plan that addresses our long-term debt must be phased in gradually—not only to protect our fragile recovery but also to give people time to adjust to the reforms. Moreover, by enacting a plan now but implementing it when the economy is stronger, we can help our economy grow in the short run by reducing uncertainty about our fiscal future by giving families, lenders, and businesses a much-needed boost in confidence. Long-term public investments in R&D, education, and infrastructure can also play an important role in boosting our economy in both the short run and the long run, particularly with interest rates as low as they are now.

After a lifetime spent working in business, government, and finance, I watch with growing alarm as today's national leaders refuse to confront our long-term debt. Year after frustrating year, Congress—which is too often partisan, petulant, paralyzed, and focused on the short run—keeps kicking the can of fiscal responsibility further down the road, to be addressed at some unspecified point in the future.

But when? And how? All the ideological "my way or the highway" rhetoric may help showboating politicians win elections in gerrymandered districts over the short term, but it's no way to reach the sort of bipartisan compromises that have traditionally enabled this nation to enact sensible policies for the common good over the long term.

Fortunately, the United States and its leaders have both the information and time necessary to turn the ship and avoid a collision with long-term debt. But we need to make plans and initiate changes soon because, given the magnitude of the challenge, last-minute swerves just won't work—economically or politically. If our leaders fail to change course in time, the unforgiving math of runaway long-term debt and compounding interest will become as destructive as the lurking, massive, unyielding iceberg that sank the "unsinkable" *Titanic*. Unfortunately, while some policymakers have begun talking more about debt, they are generally focused on a ten-year outlook, ignoring the true threat of massive debt that lies beyond the horizon.

# A PERSPECTIVE FROM THE HEARTLAND

I trace the roots of my belief in the moral imperative of fiscal responsibility to my childhood in Kearney, Nebraska, where my parents, who were Greek immigrants, ran a twenty-four-hour diner called the Central Café. For those of you unfamiliar with Kearney (perhaps that's all of you), it is a modest town on the Platte River which, when I was born in 1926, was home to about eight thousand people. When I was eight, at the height of the Great Depression, my father put me to work at the cash register, where customers settled up after eating.

In those days, the diner's most popular meal was the "Hot Beef Special"—an open-faced, white-bread sandwich featuring a pile of roast beef and mashed potatoes slathered with gravy, followed by a slice of homemade pie and a bottomless cup of coffee, all for thirty cents. A sign in the restroom, exhorting customers not to waste paper towels, read "Why Use Two When One Wipes Dry." Note the lack of a question mark. It wasn't a request; it was an admonition. And that said a lot about the economic environment we lived in—for a successful small business owner who worked seven days a week, waste simply wasn't an option.

Even though I was just a child, I took my job at the cash register seriously, because in my family, every penny counted. To give you a sense of our *economia*—that's Greek for "frugality"—we traded meals for haircuts with the local barber, took our weekly baths in succession using the same bathwater, and dropped whatever Lincoln pennies and Buffalo nickels we could into a piggy bank to pay for a college education that, from my perspective, lay unimaginably far away. At the time, I resented the discipline my father imposed, but many years later, I came to appreciate the thrift and spirit of community that the Great Depression had instilled.

Despite their frugality, my parents were also generous and philanthropic toward others. For decades they regularly sent money back to their home villages in Greece along with boxes of clothes and other necessities. Friends and relatives in Greece were really struggling just to get by and my parents did what they could to help. And they always gave free meals to the hungry men and women in Kearney who, because they didn't have work or money, lined up at the back door of the diner looking to do odd jobs. In all the years I lived in Kearney, I don't remember anyone ever being turned away hungry from the Central Café.

Looking back, the example my parents set for me was both clear and wise: have compassion for the poor, avoid debt whenever possible, and in the good times, save as much as possible because good times never last forever. Obviously, in the years since, I have come to appreciate that there are big differences in financing households, businesses, and nations. Working in the White House, in industry, and on Wall Street, I developed an understanding of finance in both the public and private sectors, and how the significant investments we make in education, public infrastructure, R&D, and industry pay big dividends over time. Such long-term investments can also make sense in times like these when interest rates are near historic lows and the economy could use a boost. That said, it remains true that as a guiding principle, *economia*—frugality—should remain vitally important to our nation's future, just as it was for my family as we worked so hard to bootstrap our way to the American Dream.

Whether you're an individual or a country, it's all too easy to spend other people's money. And in the case of the United States, we're going to have to keep borrowing money—much of it from lenders in other countries—to fund our projected spending. Ultimately, all of this money will have to be paid back, with interest. And who's going to be footing that bill? Sadly, unless we abandon our "buy now, pay later" mentality, it's going to be our children, grandchildren, and great-grandchildren. Burdening them with our debt is not fair or moral.

# WHAT CAN AMERICA DO TO REDUCE LONG-TERM DEBT?

In 2008, I launched the Foundation to raise awareness and inspire action to do something about America's looming long-term debt collision. In 2010, the Foundation conducted a survey of former senior economic policymakers from both parties. A resounding 100 percent of Republican and Democratic respondents agreed that America's long-term fiscal path is unsustainable. I found this unanimity at least somewhat encouraging.

Of course, I realize that it's much easier politically to acknowledge problems when you are like me and you don't have to worry about getting reelected or reappointed. By any measure, tackling the long-term debt challenge is very tough, both politically and economically. This is particularly the case at a time when our economy is still struggling and many people— some unemployed for long periods—are still looking for jobs. Many lawmakers acknowledge our long-term fiscal challenges, yet still oppose discussing debt reform now, arguing that this is the time to focus all of our efforts on reviving *today's* economy, that we can focus on the long-term debt "later." I believe this is a false choice. We can do both. Policymakers should plan and agree now for the steps that must be taken to improve our long-term fiscal outlook, but phase in those changes gradually after the short-term economic climate has improved.

# PUTTING TWO SACRED COWS OF IDEOLOGY OUT TO PASTURE

What are the main obstacles preventing such a practical, bipartisan plan to tackle our long-term debt? There are two principal ideological sacred cows that currently stand in the way of necessary reforms.

## *Sacred Cow #1: No New Taxes*

The problem at one end of the political spectrum is the ideological rigidity of many conservatives: no tax increases, no matter what. This rigidity—which has become something of an ideological obsession—is neither realistic nor responsible. For any comprehensive fiscal plan to be successful and sustained by future Congresses over the long run, it must be bipartisan. And to garner support from Democrats, it's obvious that any fiscal plan must have at least some of the deficit reduction come from an increase in revenue. So while the preference of conservatives may be to solve the debt problem without any new revenue, it's just not politically realistic.

Some of them claim that any new revenue will do damage to the economy. I personally believe that an agreement on a comprehensive fiscal plan that stabilizes the debt would be a big boost to the economy, even if it includes some revenue increases. The economy today is lacking confidence and certainty, and showing the world that America is getting its fiscal house in order would help on both counts. Remember the 1990s? We cut spending and adjusted the tax burden—in part by increasing taxes on the well-to-do. We had one of the strongest periods of economic growth in our recent history.

While many Republicans predicted that the revenue increases resulting from the Clinton-era taxes would kill the economy, the next seven years proved to be very prosperous. Unemployment fell, home ownership rose, the economy grew, and budget deficits were transformed into budget surpluses.

## Sacred Cow #2: Don't Touch My Entitlements

Meanwhile, some progressives on the opposite side of the political spectrum insist that cutting entitlements should be off-limits. This ideological rigidity doesn't square with reality any more than conservative fixations about no tax increases. Growth in entitlement programs account for literally 100 percent of the projected growth of future noninterest spending—the long-term structural spending problem is not caused by any other part of the budget. So we simply cannot successfully address our long-term debt issues without addressing entitlement reform.

# SHARED CONTRIBUTIONS

Addressing the long-term debt in a comprehensive fashion that has lasting bipartisan support will require difficult decisions that balance many competing needs and will require widespread contributions. If we were to reduce long-term U.S. debt through spending cuts alone, as some conservatives insist, such cuts would have to be so large and so painful to so many different people that such a plan would be politically impossible to get through Congress. Similarly, if we were to reduce long-term U.S. debt through tax increases alone, as some progressives suggest, such hikes would also have to be of a magnitude that they, too, would be politically impossible to enact.

Given these fiscal and political realities, I believe that the best way to achieve a comprehensive and lasting approach to stabilizing our long-term debt is with a mix of spending cuts and revenue increases in a reasonable and gradual approach. In my mind, such a plan is the only viable way to marshal the bipartisan support that would be necessary to actually get the job done and have it hold for the long run.

Such compromises will, of course, be very difficult. As the last several years of battles over the Affordable Care Act reveal, healthcare reform is highly divisive and especially complex. Negotiations over Social Security reform will no doubt also be tough. Despite this reluctance, we have little choice but to tackle these issues.

Sadly, if partisan gridlock precludes serious entitlement and tax reform for too long, our nation might eventually confront the kind of fiscal, political, and moral crunch in which politics gets even more brutal. If that happens, even the indispensable safety net for the most vulnerable could be in jeopardy because our resources would be severely constrained by soaring interest payments.

I know there are a few—and I hope it is a very few—who may not favor a safety net at all. Despite the intervening decades, I can still see those men and women lined up behind my parents' diner, hungry and looking for work. They weren't looking for a handout, but rather a hand up.

My good fortune in life was only possible due to the opportunities afforded me by a strong and healthy economy and our American democracy. In light of the growing gap between rich and poor in the United States, I believe that the most fortunate must be willing to shoulder a significantly greater burden—both in increased taxes and lower benefits—as we seek to address long-term debt—and the safety net for the most vulnerable should be fully protected and preserved.

At the same time, I cannot countenance those who refuse to compromise on entitlements, even as demographics and simple math make current policy untenable over the long term. Yes, we must tackle entitlement reform with care and compassion. But it is only through entitlement reform—coupled with strategic reductions in defense spending and increased revenue—that we can shift resources from consumption to long-term investments of the sort that will refuel the engine of economic mobility for tens of millions of Americans who now find themselves stalled in their pursuit of prosperity, progress, and the American Dream. By taking steps to address these challenges, our political leaders would give American families, lenders, and

businesses hope—and a much needed shot of confidence—
that can help stimulate the economy today and offer our children new opportunities for tomorrow.

## ADDRESSING OUR LONG-TERM DEBT
## CRISIS IS A MORAL IMPERATIVE

I am deeply troubled by America's growing income inequality
and the declining opportunities for tens of millions of my
fellow citizens to work themselves and their families into a
better position. This is not the kind of America that my generation inherited, and it's not the kind of America I want to
leave behind. The theologian Dietrich Bonhoeffer observed
that the ultimate test of a moral society is the kind of world
it leaves to its children. By that measure, leaving our children
with $62 trillion of long-term, unfunded promises would be
a profoundly immoral act, a strip-mining of the American
Dream. Yet that is the ugly inheritance we are currently
creating—unless we take action soon.

In 1912, had the captain and crew of the *Titanic* heeded
the clear warnings of ice around them rather than maintaining a high cruising speed with the ship's orchestra playing,
the dining room aglitter, and almost everyone aboard oblivi-
ous to their approaching peril, the luxury liner likely would
have completed its maiden voyage to great fanfare in New
York Harbor—a day late, perhaps, but delivering every pas-
senger safely ashore. But as history actually happened, bad

leadership—essentially, a refusal to address dangers over the horizon—led to disaster.

# A TIME FOR CHOOSING

With this stark lesson in mind, the question becomes: Will today's leaders and the public at large continue to ignore the threat of long-term debt not far over the horizon, and keep racing toward a collision with fiscal reality? Or recognizing the dangers ahead, will we slow down, adjust course, make the tough choices, and navigate toward brighter horizons of expanding possibility and prosperity? This choice is ours to make, especially because we're the ones who are creating our own long-term problems. Fortunately, we still have some time to act, but not much. Year by year, time is growing shorter.

Now in my ninth decade, I look back at my life and know that I have been an extraordinarily fortunate beneficiary of the American Dream. I am determined that future generations of Americans, including the sons and daughters of immigrants like my parents, should enjoy the same opportunity to pursue their own visions of the American Dream. Frankly, to scuttle this opportunity for future Americans would be a supreme act of selfishness and a breaking of the faith that has always sustained and strengthened our nation from generation to generation.

So now we confront a time for choosing. Together, we must chart another course—one that addresses fundamental questions about what we want our government to provide, how much we are willing to pay for it, and who will foot the bill. Ultimately, it will require a renewed focus on saving and investment over consumption and borrowing, and on paying our own way rather than borrowing from our grandchildren's future, and from our great-grandchildren's too. We have had a lot of trouble exercising this sort of long-term fiscal discipline in recent years, but it's a discipline we must embrace with new determination.

Making the necessary, tough choices will undoubtedly be difficult. Nevertheless, as someone who has seen this nation overcome nearly a century of challenges, I'm confident that we can once again make hard decisions with intelligence, wisdom, determination, and compassion. But we must start now because with every passing year of inaction, the iceberg of our own undoing only grows bigger, closer, and more dangerous.

# 1

## DECLINE INTO DEBT

### How the U.S. Economy
### Drifted Off Course

I n the 1960s, when I was CEO of Bell & Howell—at that time one of the nation's leading audio-visual equipment manu-facturers—America's labor force was the best educated and most highly trained in the world. Bolstered by the post–World War II GI Bill, which educated 7.8 million Americans, and supported by big investments in R&D and infrastructure, this American workforce could out-innovate and out-produce competitors from every other country on earth. As a result, the American middle class grew in tandem with the nation's economy and prospered as never before. For many American families, those postwar decades defined the American Dream.

How times have changed. Today, that same American Dream seems out of reach for tens of millions of hardworking families. What happened? What can we do to revive the opportunities, innovation, and competitiveness that have always made America great? And how does all of this relate to solving our long-term debt crisis?

## INCOME IS STAGNATING, MOBILITY IS LOW, AND THE GAP BETWEEN RICH AND POOR IS GROWING

To begin with, after the early 1970s, the real income growth that fueled broad American prosperity slowed dramatically. This slowdown has been acutely felt by America's middle class, whose real inflation-adjusted income has been growing slowly for more than thirty years—a generation of lost opportunity. Between 1950 and 1975, the real median income of families climbed by 93 percent. But from 1975 to 2000, it grew only by 27 percent. And since 2000, it has declined by 7 percent. In 2013, real family income was no higher than it was in 1997.

Moreover, most of the modest gains in family income that have occurred since 1975 were the result of more women entering the workforce and modest increases in their wages. Shockingly, the real median income of men in 2013 was no higher than it was in 1969—more than forty years of no growth.

The core of the American Dream has always been that if you work hard and play by the rules, you can create a better life for yourself and your family. But the public's confidence in the American Dream has taken a big hit in recent years. Ac-

## THE MEDIAN REAL INCOME FOR FAMILIES IN THE UNITED STATES TODAY IS NO HIGHER THAN IT WAS IN 1997

**Median Family Income** (2012 dollars)

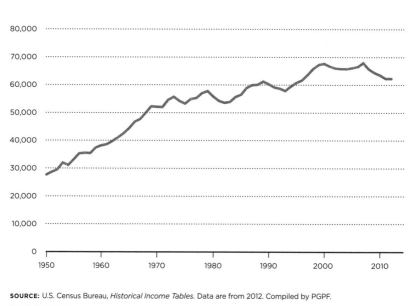

SOURCE: U.S. Census Bureau, *Historical Income Tables*. Data are from 2012. Compiled by PGPF.

cording to a Gallup poll, only 54 percent of Americans believe that it is possible "to get ahead by working hard"—down sharply from the 77 percent who held that view in 2002.

As the son of immigrant parents who worked seven days a week running a twenty-four-hour diner so that I could go to college and pursue my own ambitions, I *lived* this dream. And I believe that this possibility to work your way up should be every American's birthright, as it has been for generations.

But too often, the income group Americans are born into is the one they stay in for the rest of their lives. According to the

## THE MEDIAN REAL INCOME FOR MEN IN THE UNITED STATES HAS NOT IMPROVED OVER THE PAST SEVERAL DECADES

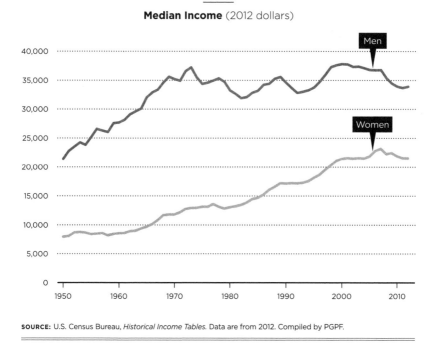

**Median Income** (2012 dollars)

**SOURCE:** U.S. Census Bureau, *Historical Income Tables.* Data are from 2012. Compiled by PGPF.

Pew Charitable Trusts, 43 percent of those born into the lowest income quintile stay there as adults, and another 27 percent never get beyond the next income quintile. Research by Professor Miles Corak shows that income mobility for American families is also low compared with other leading nations.

As the following chart indicates, the United States currently ranks thirteenth in income mobility among sixteen advanced nations. This is especially disturbing given that the United States also has the second-highest proportion of children living in poverty among thirty-five developed countries.

# THE UNITED STATES RANKS ONLY THIRTEENTH IN INCOME MOBILITY FROM ONE GENERATION TO THE NEXT

### Intergenerational Income Mobility

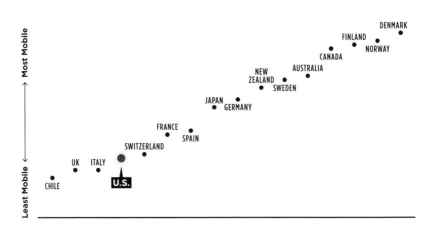

**SOURCE:** Miles Corak, *Inequality from Generation to Generation: The United States in Comparison,* 2012. Compiled by PGPF.
**NOTE:** Mobility is measured as intergenerational earnings elasticity, an indicator of how closely children's earnings are related to those of their parents. In low-mobility countries, children's earnings in adulthood depend heavily on their parents' earnings. Consequently, children of low-earning parents almost always grow up to have low earnings while the children of high-earning parents almost always grow up to have high earnings.

Opportunities for young people, especially minorities and those who have low incomes, are also distressingly scarce, and too many young people lack the skills that employers need. Among people aged twenty to twenty-four, the unemployment rate was 12.8 percent in 2013. The opportunities for people with poor educational backgrounds are similarly limited. The unemployment rate of people without a high school diploma was 10.9 percent in 2013—almost three times the unemployment rate of people with a college degree. And single mothers had unemployment rates of 10.2 percent in 2013—more than double the rate of married women.

Over roughly the same period that incomes have been stagnating and mobility has been low, America led a revolution in computer and information processing technology. A typical smartphone now boasts more computing power than that which guided the Apollo spacecraft, and the Internet has transformed the way billions of people search for information, socialize, and do business. As computing power, speed, and usage soared, routine tasks that had been performed by low-skill workers in earlier years became automated—a process that continues even today. These technological advances enabled many manufacturing firms to produce goods with fewer workers and to communicate instantly with overseas plants to coordinate planning, production, and shipping—more and more of which is automated, even overseas. As a result, since 1980, the number of manufacturing jobs in the United States has fallen by about seven million. Meanwhile, demand for high-skill workers with the ability to design, program, and use these new technologies soared. While real wages for these Americans climbed significantly, real wages for middle-skill workers stagnated and those for low-skill workers fell. So even as overall labor productivity has doubled since 1980, the economic benefit to those unable to adapt to the new technologies has been limited at best.

To compensate for income stagnation—and in part because of a "buy now, pay later" mentality fueled by easy credit—millions of Americans started saving less and borrowing more.

At the peak of the housing boom in the mid-2000s, homeowners were extracting $800 billion a year in equity from their homes—up from $300 billion in 2000, according to research by Alan Greenspan and James Kennedy. For many, the subsequent collapse in housing and equity prices turned owning a home, long a key element of the American Dream, into something closer to a nightmare.

Personal saving rates in America have fallen substantially over the past forty years, and we save significantly less than citizens in other major countries. Without personal savings, too many households do not have enough wealth for a com-

## THE U.S. PERSONAL SAVING RATE HAS FALLEN SHARPLY OVER THE PAST FORTY YEARS AND REMAINS LOW AT 4.5 PERCENT

**Personal Saving** (Percentage of disposable income)

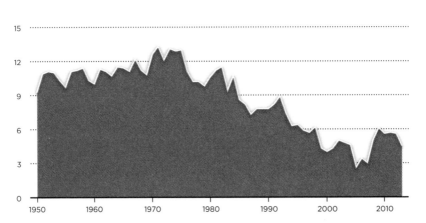

**SOURCE:** Bureau of Economic Analysis, *National Income and Product Accounts Tables,* May 2014. Compiled by PGPF.

fortable retirement, for their kids' education, for unanticipated expenses, or for an unexpected loss in family income.

Because many Americans count their homes as their primary asset, the nosedive in home values had a devastating effect on the net worth of many families. The Federal Reserve reports that real net worth for the median family fell almost 40 percent between 2007 and 2010—to levels last seen in the early 1990s. The modest recovery in home prices since the depths of the recession has reversed some of this decline in net worth, but for millions who lost their homes to foreclosure, great damage has been done.

With middle-class wages stagnant (and low-skill wages falling), millions of hardworking people have had trouble covering their daily household expenses, let alone saving for the future. Meanwhile, a fortunate few have more than they ever had before. This divergence in fortunes has produced a widening income gap between the haves and have-nots. As the following chart indicates, real after-tax incomes among the most prosperous 1 percent of all households soared between 1979 and 2010 while the incomes of middle-class households hardly budged by comparison. This growing disparity is unhealthy for our democracy.

Clearly, the effect of the postcrash recovery has been very inequitable. In the first three years of the economic recovery, 95 percent of the income gains went to the top 1 percent of the income spectrum, according to UC-Berkeley professor Emmanuel Saez. This unprecedented inequality is an important reason why I believe the well-to-do must share fully in the effort and the sacrifice to get our fiscal house in order.

## ALTHOUGH THE INCOMES OF THE WEALTHY ARE VOLATILE, THEY HAVE GROWN MUCH FASTER THAN THE INCOMES OF OTHER GROUPS

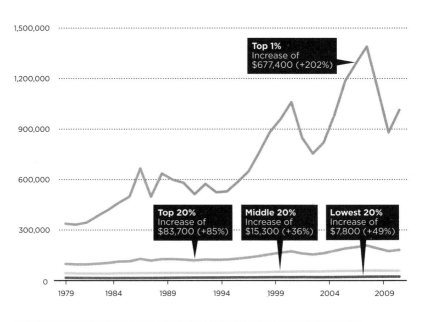

**Average Annual After-Tax Income** (2010 dollars)

Top 1%
Increase of
$677,400 (+202%)

Top 20%
Increase of
$83,700 (+85%)

Middle 20%
Increase of
$15,300 (+36%)

Lowest 20%
Increase of
$7,800 (+49%)

**SOURCE:** Congressional Budget Office, *The Distribution of Household Income and Federal Taxes, 2010,* December 2013. Compiled by PGPF.

## COMPETITION FROM EMERGING MARKETS IS RISING RAPIDLY

Over the past two decades, the world has witnessed a truly remarkable period of economic growth, which saw a rapid expansion of emerging economies in Asia and South America. This growth has lifted hundreds of millions of people in the developing world out of poverty, reduced production costs for

U.S. companies, and lowered the price of many goods for U.S. consumers.

But this development has also brought new challenges for the United States because the world is now much more competitive in many important sectors. It used to be that only the simplest of products—shoes and textiles, for example—were made by emerging countries on any significant scale. Not so today. Emerging markets such as China and India are major producers of not just basic goods but vehicles, appliances, and sophisticated electronics components, including semiconductors, LCD panels, and high-efficiency wind and solar equipment. In 1991, the

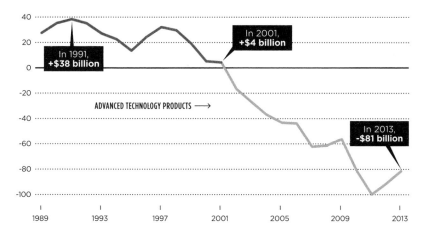

## THE UNITED STATES HAS GONE FROM A TRADE SURPLUS TO A TRADE DEFICIT IN ADVANCED TECHNOLOGY PRODUCTS

**Trade Balance** (Billions of dollars)

In 1991, +$38 billion

In 2001, +$4 billion

ADVANCED TECHNOLOGY PRODUCTS ⟶

In 2013, -$81 billion

**SOURCE:** U.S. Census Bureau, *Trade in Goods with Advance Technology Products,* February 2014. Compiled by PGPF.
**NOTE:** Advanced technology products include robots, semiconductors, laser printers, and other sophisticated electronic goods.

United States ran a $38 billion trade surplus in advanced technology products such as MRI machines and lasers. By 2013, that high-tech surplus had become an $81 billion deficit.

Just as the United States was the world's engine of economic growth during the twentieth century, emerging markets are now generating most of the world's growth, accounting for 68 percent of global economic growth in 2012—up from 43 percent in 2000. Although some emerging countries are currently facing some choppy economic waters, few would question the remarkable gains these countries have made in just the past twenty years—and the important role they will likely continue to play over the next twenty years.

China alone has increased its share of the world's fixed investment (such as factories and manufacturing equipment) from 2 percent in 1990 to 22 percent today. By contrast, the U.S. share has fallen from 24 percent in 1990 to 18 percent today. Given the role of investment in growth, it's not surprising that since 1990, China has quadrupled its share of annual global economic activity to about 16 percent. The U.S. share was 20 percent in 1990 and is at 16 percent today.

One revealing indicator of China's economic development is the country's increased emphasis on protecting its own intellectual property. Even as we read news reports of Chinese manufacturers producing counterfeit products—from luxury handbags to Apple electronics—it is also investing heavily in patenting its own innovations. According to the World Intellectual Property Organization (WIPO), the number of applications to China's patent office increased about 35 percent from 2010 to 2011—surpassing the number of patent applica-

## CHINA HAS RAPIDLY SURPASSED THE REST OF THE WORLD IN THE NUMBER OF PATENT APPLICATIONS SUBMITTED

**Total Patent Applications**

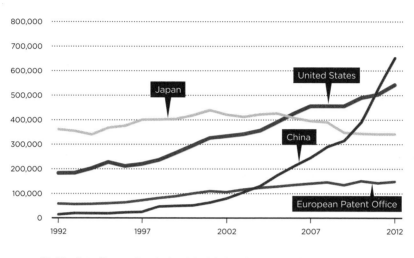

**SOURCE:** World Intellectual Property Organization, *IP Statistics Data Center,* January 2014. Compiled by PGPF.

tions to the U.S. Patent and Trademark Office. To be sure, the quality of the Chinese patents may not match U.S. patents. But as WIPO's director general wrote in its 2012 annual report, "though caution is required in directly comparing IP filing figures across countries, these trends nevertheless reflect how the geography of innovation has shifted."

For many years, America led the world in initial public offerings (IPOs) of start-up companies, which have historically been a major source of innovation and new U.S. jobs. Yet in 2011, Chinese companies raised almost twice as much IPO capital as U.S. companies did, according to data collected by

Ernst and Young. This gap portends even greater competition in the years ahead, and precisely in the arenas that have always been our strength.

The hard truth is that the United States also does not invest as much as many other developed countries do. In 2007 (the peak of the last business cycle), net investment in the United States (as a share of GDP) was lower than in twenty-one (out of thirty-three) other developed countries.

These growing competitive challenges mean that we will need to invest more to ensure that we are giving our people the education, skills, infrastructure, research and development, and general tools they need to invent new products. We need to invest in ways that create enough new jobs paying wages that enable people to get ahead from year to year, and from generation to generation. In other words, we need to equip ourselves to compete in new ways in today's knowledge-based, technological world and—through that transformation—reignite the income growth that has always made the American Dream more than just an ideal, but an achievable reality.

But where will we get the resources to make those investments? As I mentioned earlier, household saving rates have fallen sharply over the past fifty years. But households aren't the only ones whose saving has fallen. Saving by our federal government has also been on a long-term decline as a result of rising budget deficits. (Our federal budget deficit is what economists call "negative saving.") Indeed, when saving from all sectors of the economy is combined—households, governments, and businesses—a distressing trend emerges: the national saving rate in the United States has declined significantly since the 1960s. Moreover, we have had one of the lowest national saving rates among advanced countries since 2000. Even when the economy was at its last business-cycle peak in 2007, our net national saving rate was the fifth lowest among thirty-two developed countries—only above Portugal, Greece, Iceland, and Hungary—according to the Organization for Economic Cooperation and Development (OECD).

## COMPARED WITH OTHER MAJOR COUNTRIES, THE UNITED STATES HAS HAD A LOW NATIONAL SAVING RATE

**Net National Saving Rate** (Percentage of GDP)

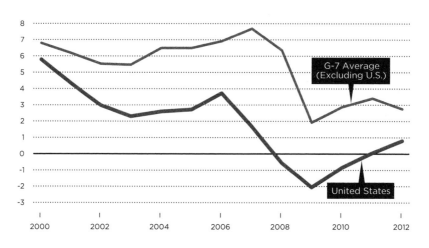

**SOURCE:** Organization for Economic Cooperation and Development, *National Accounts at a Glance,* April 2014. Compiled by PGPF.
**NOTE:** The G-7 is a group of seven advanced economies: Canada, France, Germany, Italy, Japan, the UK, and the United States.

# THE U.S. NATIONAL SAVING RATE HAS DECLINED SIGNIFICANTLY SINCE THE MID-1960s

Net National Saving (Percentage of GNI)

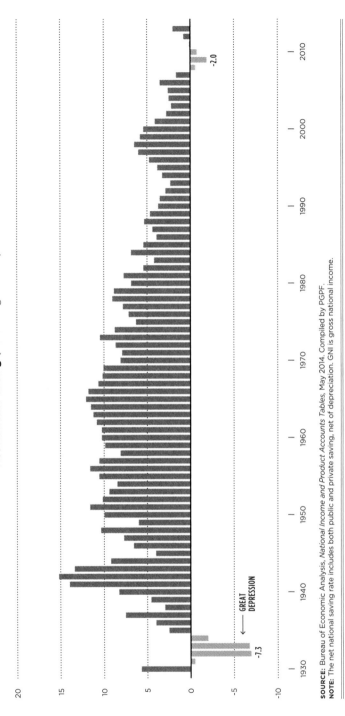

GREAT DEPRESSION

-7.3

-2.0

SOURCE: Bureau of Economic Analysis, *National Income and Product Accounts Tables*, May 2014. Compiled by PGPF.
NOTE: The net national saving rate includes both public and private saving, net of depreciation. GNI is gross national income.

# TRANSFORMING AMERICAN EDUCATION IS AN IMPERATIVE

Education is absolutely vital to America's ability to remain a first-rate competitive country in an increasingly technological and knowledge-based world economy. Educating future generations will require not just adequate funding, but also a fundamental transformation to ensure that students are learning at world-class levels, and that American workers have skills that are in high demand. Improving educational effectiveness, particularly in math and science, needs to be nothing less than a national imperative.

Today, it's clear that many other countries have surpassed us in educational and skills achievement. Despite the fact that we spend about 40 percent more per pupil on primary and secondary education than other advanced countries do on average, our high school students actually score below average in math and have only middling scores in science and reading. According the OECD, U.S. students in 2012 ranked twenty-seventh in math, twentieth in science, and seventeenth in reading among thirty-four developed nations. To remain competitive, we need to boost those scores substantially.

There are a variety of reasons why American students underperform relative to their peers in other countries, but in my view one factor does not get enough attention: too many children, especially in poor and urban areas from single-parent households, are unprepared for school. According to the OECD, the United States ranks twenty-eighth out of thirty-three developed countries in the preschool enrollment rate for four-year-olds in both public and private institutions. The enrollment rate of four-year-olds in the United States—about 75 percent—is the same as in Russia, but much lower than in Spain, Mexico, Denmark, and Japan. And in terms of resource allocation, the U.S. government spends less on early childhood education, relative to its GDP, than twenty-one other OECD nations—including Mexico, Poland, and the Czech Republic.

Pre-K education—especially with parental involvement—can pay big dividends. The mere presence of books in a household is highly correlated with a child's future educational attainment even after controlling for the family's income and level of education.* Parents can play a big role by simply reading to their children. However, statistics show that parents below the poverty line are less likely than nonpoor parents to read to their children every day.

Economic research from Professor James Heckman from the University of Chicago—who shared the Nobel Prize in Economics in 2000—shows that early childhood education can have a very important effect on student achievement later in life. Although some of the benefits of early education fade with time, important benefits seem to persist into adulthood, as shown by lower rates of welfare dependency and criminal activity.†

---

*M.D.R. Evans, Jonathan Kelley, Joanna Sikora, Donald J. Treiman, "Family Scholarly Culture, and Educational Success: Books and Schooling in 27 Nations," *Research in Social Stratification and Mobility* 28, no. 2 (June 2010): 171–97.

†James J. Heckman, "Schools, Skills, and Synapses," *Economic Inquiry* 46, no. 3 (July 2008): 289–324.

A number of innovative programs for early childhood education have emerged recently. For example, some promising work has been supported by foundations such as the Buffett Early Childhood Fund. This fund is working to promote state-of-the-art "Educare" schools that help prepare at-risk young children from poor families for elementary school and promote best practices in the field of early childhood education.

Given our wealth and educational infrastructure, the United States should also lead the world in the share of young people with college degrees. But in 2010, twelve developed nations had a larger share of young adults with college degrees than the United States did. While 42 percent of America's young adults have earned college degrees, that figure is 57 percent in Canada and Japan and 65 percent in Korea.

Engineering and science are critical backgrounds for today's growing, innovative, technological, and competitive global economy. Yet only 16 percent of U.S. undergraduate degrees are in engineering or natural sciences, compared with 23 percent in Europe, 31 percent in Asia, and 44 percent in China.

According to the National Center for Education Statistics (NCES), only forty-three thousand students received degrees in computer science from U.S. universities in 2011 (the most recent data available). That's down by one fourth since 2003. This trend contributes to a mismatch between the skills available in our workforce and the skills required by employers—a mismatch that reduces employment options for workers and holds back economic growth.

## THE UNITED STATES LAGS IN THE PERCENTAGE OF UNIVERSITY STUDENTS EARNING SCIENCE AND ENGINEERING DEGREES

**Science and Engineering Degrees** (Percentage of undergraduate degrees)

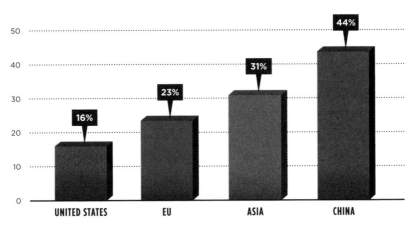

SOURCE: National Science Foundation, *Science and Engineering Indicators 2014,* February 2014. Compiled by PGPF.
NOTE: This chart includes natural sciences (physical, biological, agricultural, computer science, and mathematics) and engineering but excludes social sciences.

Currently, nearly half of the graduate students in engineering and computer science at U.S. universities are foreign-born. On the positive side, this is a great testament to America's continuing ability to attract bright students from around the world. On the negative side, it's also an example of how our primary and secondary schools, as well as colleges, are failing to engage, prepare, or motivate American-born students for advanced degrees in the technical fields on which the new economy thrives. Even worse, about a quarter of the foreign-born engineers and scientists trained in our universities take their talents back to their home countries in the first year after graduating, in part because our flawed immigration system makes it too difficult for them to remain in the United States.

According to Walter Isaacson's biography of the late Apple cofounder Steve Jobs, one of the reasons Apple has opened factories in China is because there are more trained engineers available in that country. Jobs noted that Apple needed thirty thousand engineers to support its seven hundred thousand manufacturing workers in China, and he just couldn't find that many engineers to hire in the United States. This is not just an embarrassment, but a lost opportunity; in an increasingly knowledge- and skill-based competitive global economy, we simply must ensure that our workers have the education and skills employers need.

The high levels of long-term unemployment—and the erosion of skills it entails—is another serious problem that has contributed to the skills gap and needs attention. At the end of 2013, 3.9 million people—more than the total population of the state of Connecticut—had been unemployed for more than six months. To reverse this tragic situation, we need successful training programs that can help these workers rebuild their skills for our new economy.

However, if improving educational and training outcomes was simply a function of more dollars, then we could commit to more spending. But between the mid-1980s and 2008, U.S. spending per student rose 45 percent (after adjusting for inflation), while reading scores among seventeen-year-olds dropped 1 percent and math scores barely crept up 1 percent. I'm not an education expert, and I don't pretend to have the solutions, but this much is clear: we're not getting a great return on our educational investment, and we need to figure out how our dollars can be spent more effectively to help our students acquire the knowledge, skills, and training to compete and win in a global economy. To achieve that goal, we will need a profound transformation of our educational system.

# IMPROVING INFRASTRUCTURE CRITICAL TO U.S. COMPETITIVENESS

Beginning in the late nineteenth century, superior infra-structure began to give the United States a competitive edge as it built a great industrial economy. Our robust infrastructure in railroads, bridges, highways, ports, dams, power plants, electrical transmission networks, and in recent decades, extraordinary advances in telecommunications provided a powerful platform for our economy to grow and prosper. Unfortunately, we have been coasting on past investments, even as major elements of that infrastructure have begun to wear out, and many other countries' infrastructure is now better than ours. According to the World Economic Forum (WEF), the United States now ranks sixteenth in the world for the overall quality of its infrastructure. Yes, America invented the Internet, but France, the UK, Germany, Canada, Korea, Japan, and twelve other nations have established more broadband connections per person than we have, the WEF reports.

# THE UNITED STATES RANKS ONLY SIXTEENTH IN QUALITY OF OVERALL INFRASTRUCTURE, ACCORDING TO THE WORLD ECONOMIC FORUM

## Quality of Overall Infrastructure

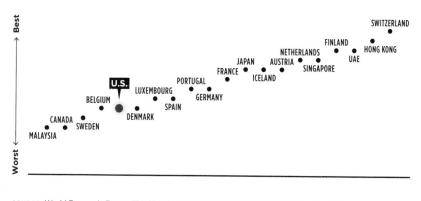

**SOURCE:** World Economic Forum, *The Global Competitiveness Report 2014-2015,* August 2014. Compiled by PGPF.
**NOTE:** The World Economic Forum score on overall infrastructure includes transport, telephony, and energy. Only the top twenty ranked countries are shown.

Similarly, while America pioneered transcontinental railroads and built the interstate highway system, our crumbling transportation network now seriously lags those of many industrial nations. According to the Texas A&M Transportation Institute, road congestion in the United States cost us $121 billion in wasted fuel and time in 2011. Over the next decade alone, that's potentially more than $1 trillion wasted—dollars that could be working for us instead of being squandered in bumper-to-bumper traffic.

To address these shortcomings, the U.S. government should increase its investment in infrastructure. Moreover, because interest rates are so low in today's economy, those long-term investments could be procured now at very low costs.

I also support the creation of a national infrastructure bank. While such a proposal enjoys support from a range of bipartisan voices in Washington, it has not yet been acted upon, and the need for investment funds is more acute than ever. The idea has been put forward in different forms over the years, but typically calls for federal funds to be used alongside private funds to finance infrastructure projects. A critical element will be requiring that private investors have enough capital at stake in the bank to ensure that they will fully share both the gains and the losses from any investment. The debacle at Fannie Mae and Freddie Mac highlighted the dangerous potential for awarding gains to the private sector while leaving the public sector on the hook for losses.

# WE NEED TO INVEST MORE
# IN OUR FUTURE

Virtually every economist agrees that in the long run there is a direct connection between how much of an economy's current income is allocated to future purposes and how fast productivity will grow over time. According to the CBO, higher debt crowds out investment, resulting in a smaller capital stock and lower output and income in the long run. As I discuss in the next chapter, unless we begin addressing our long-term debt challenge in a meaningful way, a growing and chronic lack of resources will prevent our nation from having an adequate level of long-term strategic investments that are so critical to compete successfully in a global arena. Recognizing this is critically important: as a nation, we must make bigger and smarter investments to compete in coming decades. If we don't rein in our consumption, stabilize our debt, raise saving, and start making these necessary investments, our country is going to face a sobering long-term reality.

I don't believe in the inevitability of American decline. Quite the contrary. We live in a world of rising global standards, and that's a good thing because growth and stronger competition abroad pushes us all to become smarter and better and more productive. We just need to muster the political will to make wiser policy choices, and that starts with getting our fiscal house in order—and sooner rather than later. We must avoid a collision with our own mounting and unsustainable long-term debt and release the resources we need to meet the challenges in a far more competitive world economy.

# 2

## COLLISION COURSE

### How America's Long-term Debt Could Damage Our Economy

espite partisan wrangling on Capitol Hill about our national debt, almost all of the hullabaloo has been misdirected because it has been solely focused on near-term deficits. Those noisy debates—often starring rigid ideologues preening for a narrow constituency—are endangering our country's future not only because they make legislative compromise harder to reach, but also because they distract Congress from a much more serious challenge looming over the horizon: a growing problem of debt over the long term. Like the RMS *Titanic,* whose captain and crew ignored warnings of danger ahead, America is on a collision course with a serious long-term fiscal challenge.

Just how big is long-term debt projected to become? The nonpartisan Congressional Budget Office (CBO) projects that

# U.S. DEBT HELD BY THE PUBLIC IS ON AN UNSUSTAINABLE PATH

**Debt Held by the Public** (Percentage of GDP)

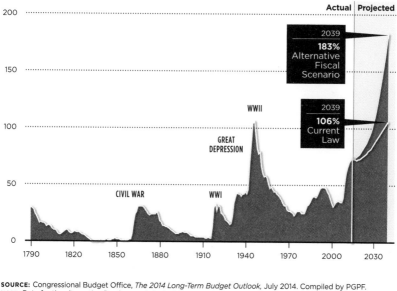

SOURCE: Congressional Budget Office, *The 2014 Long-Term Budget Outlook,* July 2014. Compiled by PGPF.
NOTE: Data for the alternative fiscal scenario includes economic feedback.

under current law, federal debt will rise to 106 percent of GDP within twenty-five years. However, those current-law projections are quite optimistic in my opinion (see Appendix II). Under an alternative fiscal scenario that makes less optimistic assumptions about future budget policy and incorporates the negative effects of debt on the economy, the CBO projects that debt could soar to a staggering 183 percent of GDP within twenty-five years.

The CBO warns in *The 2014 Long-Term Budget Outlook* that these debts even at optimistic current-law levels would damage our economy:

The high and rising amounts of federal debt held by the public that CBO projects for the coming decades under [current law] would have significant negative consequences for the economy in the long term and would impose significant constraints on future budget policy. In particular, the projected amounts of debt would reduce the total amounts of national saving and income in the long term; increase the government's interest payments, thereby putting more pressure on the rest of the budget; limit lawmakers' flexibility to respond to unforeseen events; and increase the likelihood of a fiscal crisis.

The size of our long-term debt can also be measured by the unfunded obligations and future promises expressed in today's dollars. This measure subtracts all of the future promises we've made—including Social Security, Medicare, and other spending—from the revenue we currently anticipate collecting. Then it adds those unfunded promises to the current level of our debt. By this measure, the United States faces a staggering shortfall of $62 trillion (under CBO's alternative fiscal scenario) over the next fifty years.

To be sure, every long-term projection is uncertain and no one really knows how high long-term debt will become as a percentage of GDP. But there is one undeniable truth: at some point, we will be forced to confront our long-term debt. The exact path for federal debt may be unknown, but as the CBO wrote in *The 2014 Long-Term Budget Outlook*, the federal budget is on an unsustainable path and the agency's analysis "applies under a wide range of possible values for some key factors that influence federal spending and revenues." Those key factors include assumptions about productivity growth, interest rates, and healthcare growth.

More important, uncertainty about the projected outlook of our future debt is not a valid reason for disregarding the challenges it poses. To the contrary, uncertainty is actually an argument for doing more to solve the problem of our long-term debt. In our personal lives, we have long dealt with economic uncertainty by setting aside some money for a rainy day. Economists call this "precautionary saving"—an economically rational plan to hedge against an uncertain and potentially worrisome future. To hedge against uncertainty about the exact growth rate of our debt, governments need to respond in a similar way by saving more—or equivalently by running smaller deficits, or ideally by surpluses once the economy is healthy.

## STATE AND LOCAL IMBALANCES

Our nation's debt problems are broader than just imbalances in the federal budget. State and local governments, many of which bear significant healthcare costs, also face troubling long-term fiscal shortfalls. The Peterson Foundation recently co-funded a report by the State Budget Crisis Task Force, led by former New York lieutenant governor Richard Ravitch and former Federal Reserve chairman Paul Volcker. The report this task force issued was unequivocal in declaring that states face growing budget challenges in the years ahead—and that these challenges are directly connected to some of the same factors that are putting such pressure on the federal budget. For instance, as a result of rising healthcare costs, states are now spending more on Medicaid than on elementary and secondary education combined.

## PROJECTED HEALTH EXPENDITURES OF STATE AND LOCAL GOVERNMENTS INDICATE CROWDING OUT OF NONHEALTH SPENDING

**Expenditures of State and Local Governments**
(Percentage of GDP)

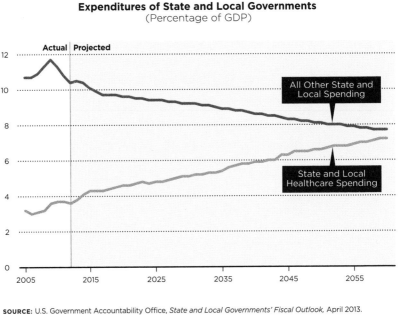

SOURCE: U.S. Government Accountability Office, *State and Local Governments' Fiscal Outlook,* April 2013. Compiled by PGPF.

States are also reducing real spending per student at their public colleges and universities—precisely the type of investment that produces scientific breakthroughs and a well-educated and competitive workforce. As the federal government considers ways to reduce its own healthcare costs, states worry that the costs will be shifted to them and cause them to cut other services even further.

Meanwhile, many pension plans for state employees are currently in dire financial straits. All told, the states face unfunded pension and retiree healthcare liabilities of between $1 trillion and $3 trillion, according to the State Budget Crisis Task Force. For too long now, creative accounting—what we might also call political accounting—has triumphed over honest transparency about the real magnitude of these liabilities.

Similar challenges are also pervasive at the local level, where a bankrupt Detroit is only one example of municipalities under great fiscal distress. Such state and local crises are of national concern because they have profound implications for the delivery of some of our most important public services.

## PRIVATE-SECTOR DEBT

And let's not forget about private-sector debt either—the debts owed by consumers, households, and businesses. It was that sort of speculative, private-sector debt that helped trigger the great crash in 2008. To put the scale of this speculation into a long-term perspective, the debt of banks and other financial institutions skyrocketed from 6 percent of GDP in 1960 to nearly 120 percent in 2008.

Household debt also mushroomed from about 50 percent of GDP in 1985 to almost 95 percent in 2008. Since the 2008 downturn, many financial institutions and households have retrenched somewhat by cutting costs, writing off losses, paying down debt and—in some cases—enduring foreclosures and bankruptcies. But as the chart below shows, the total debt for all sectors in our economy—government, businesses, and households—is still more than 325 percent of GDP. When the economy gets back to normal, will we simply return to our "buy now, pay later" mentality? I fear the answer is yes.

## DEBT LEVELS HAVE RISEN IN MANY SECTORS OF THE ECONOMY

**Debt Outstanding** (Percentage of GDP)

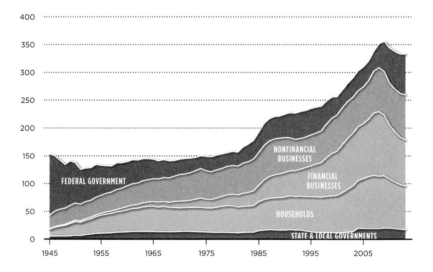

**SOURCE:** Board of Governors of the Federal Reserve System, *Financial Accounts of the United States,* June 2014, and Bureau of Economic Analysis, *National Income and Product Accounts Tables,* June 2014. Compiled by PGPF.

# ECONOMIC COSTS OF RISING
# LONG-TERM DEBT

The effects of excessive debt in the long run are widespread and profound. Although a weak economy has prompted the Federal Reserve to keep interest rates very low for several years, a recovering economy will eventually lead to an increase in rates. Once the economy is back to full employment, rising debts will begin to put upward pressure on interest rates and slow the growth of income. Those higher interest rates will make everything we pay for with borrowed money more expensive, from homes to cars to a college education. And slowing income growth will make it even harder for Americans to get ahead.

Unfortunately, a steady erosion of growth in living standards may actually be the *best* of the bad consequences stemming from the government's soaring debt trajectory. That's because history suggests something far worse is possible: a catastrophic fiscal crisis. Although there is no clear threshold trigger, numerous scholars and economists from respected U.S. and international institutions have shown that as debt rises to excessive levels, economic growth can slow dramatically and the risk of a sudden fiscal crisis increases.

Even if we manage to escape a sudden crisis, we may face a daunting and long-lasting alternative: a persistent "slow-growth" economy. This is a situation in which persistent deficits and ballooning interest payments crowd out future-oriented investments by the public and private sectors for years at a time. That's because when the government increases debt over the long run, it absorbs funds from financial markets that companies would otherwise invest in factories, equipment, and innovation. Though public-sector investment is a smaller part of our economy, it is also vitally important for funding truly long-term priorities such as education and training, basic scientific research, and major infrastructure like roads, ports, and airports. It's those types of investments—which pay dividends over time—that will be crowded out as interest costs on the debt consume an escalating share of the federal budget.

America's interest costs are already on a pace to march upward as the economy recovers and interest rates rise to traditional levels. Over the next ten years, interest payments are projected to be $5.2 trillion under current law and $5.6 trillion under the alternative fiscal scenario. Over the long run, they are staggering. In 2013, interest costs were 1.3 percent of GDP. But by 2050, they are expected to be between 5.6 percent of GDP (under current law) and 10.7 percent of GDP (under the alternative fiscal scenario). At 10.7 percent, interest costs would be four times what the federal government typically spends each year on education, R&D, and nondefense infrastructure *combined*.

Those projections assume that interest rates on government debt rise to 4.8 percent. If interest rates rose to 6.8 percent instead—about two thirds of what they were during the 1980s— interest costs over the next ten years would rise from $5.6 trillion to $8.3 trillion under the budget assumptions of the alternative fiscal scenario. By 2050, they would be a staggering 22 percent of GDP.

If investments in our future are akin to a boat that takes us places, then interest payments are like a hole in the bottom of

## BY 2050, INTEREST COSTS ON THE DEBT ARE PROJECTED TO BE FOUR TIMES WHAT THE FEDERAL GOVERNMENT HAS HISTORICALLY SPENT ON EDUCATION, R&D, AND INFRASTRUCTURE COMBINED

**Federal Spending** (Percentage of GDP)

| | | | |
|---|---|---|---|
| **2.7%** | **1.3%** | **7.0%** | **10.7%** |
| R&D | | | |
| INFRASTRUCTURE | | | |
| EDUCATION | | | |
| (1964–2013) | 2014 | 2039 | 2050 |
| **Average Spending** | | Interest Costs | |

Alternative Fiscal Scenario

Current Law

**SOURCE:** Congressional Budget Office, *The 2014 Long-Term Budget Outlook,* July 2014, and Office of Management and Budget, *Budget of the United States Government, Fiscal Year 2015,* March 2014. Compiled by PGPF.
**NOTE:** Infrastructure excludes defense. Data for the alternative fiscal scenario does not include economic feedback.

that boat—a growing problem whose consequences only get worse until the hole is repaired. That's because interest payments are largely about the past, not the future—especially as they compound. They represent the long, expensive tail of spending and borrowing decisions made long ago that will burden our nation in coming decades. To prosper in a far more competitive and knowledge-based global economy, America will need to ramp up its investments.

Nearly everybody agrees on the importance of more investment, but too few have confronted the question: Where will we get the resources to fund it? Without those resources, we will have trouble launching the bold initiatives that spurred American innovation in the past. We have prospered as a nation in part because we had the vision and resources to take on big projects, such as building the interstate highway system, exploring space, developing the Internet, and mapping the human genome.

A country under grave economic duress does not have the resources to lead the world economically or the stature or credibility to serve as a policy exemplar. Are we prepared to cede global leadership to another power, such as China? Worse, will we gradually cede—through our own lack of fiscal discipline—control over our own domestic and foreign affairs to the overseas creditors holding our debt? Already, as the chart on the next page illustrates, about half of our publicly held debt is owned by foreign investors, with a large share of that held by China and Japan.

Luckily, our fiscal dysfunction has yet to induce any major negative repercussions from international markets. In fact, interest rates have fallen to near-record lows. But this does not necessarily reflect increasing confidence in the United States. Rather, it is the result of a recession, slow economic recovery, massive quantitative easing (the Federal Reserve buying U.S. bonds), and a significant flight away from higher-risk sovereign bonds in Europe and riskier assets in general. Interest payments on the national debt are about what they were before the recession, but that's only because interest

# NEARLY HALF OF U.S. DEBT IS OWNED BY FOREIGNERS

**2014**

U.S. HOLDINGS 52%

FOREIGN HOLDINGS 48%

| COUNTRY | MAY 2014 | |
| --- | --- | --- |
| | HOLDINGS (in billions of U.S. dollars) | HOLDINGS (as a percentage of U.S. debt held by the public) |
| China | $1,270.9 | 10.1 percent |
| Japan | $1,220.1 | 9.7 percent |
| Belgium | $362.4 | 2.9 percent |
| Caribbean Banking Centers | $310.8 | 2.5 percent |
| Oil Exporters | $257.9 | 2.1 percent |
| All Other Countries | $2,553.9 | 20.4 percent |
| **Total Foreign Holdings** | **$5,976.0** | **47.7 percent** |

**SOURCE:** U.S. Treasury, *Public Debt Report*, July 2014, and *Major Foreign Holders of Treasury Securities*, July 2014. Compiled by PGPF.
**NOTE:** U.S. debt here refers to debt held by the public. Caribbean banking centers include Bahamas, Bermuda, British Virgin Islands, Cayman Islands, Netherlands Antilles, and Panama. Oil exporters include Ecuador, Venezuela, Indonesia, Bahrain, Iran, Iraq, Kuwait, Oman, Qatar, Saudi Arabia, the United Arab Emirates, Algeria, Gabon, Libya, and Nigeria. The data in this table are collected primarily from U.S.-based custodians. Since U.S. securities held in overseas custody accounts might not be attributed to the actual owners, the data might not provide a precise accounting of individual country ownership of Treasury securities.

rates are currently so low. Today's debt is more than double what it was in 2006, and when interest rates rise again, we're in for a rude awakening.

One very important reason we have been spared the full cost of rising debt is because the U.S. dollar is a global reserve currency, which makes assets denominated in dollars sought-after securities around the world. While some see that status as our salvation, I worry that this perception just gives us a longer rope with which to hang ourselves.

If markets were to lose faith in U.S. debt and investors sought to dump their dollar assets, the value of the dollar would plummet and interest rates and inflation would climb precipitously, pushing not just the United States but the entire global economy into an economic crisis. The effects could be large: the world is awash in dollars and dollar-denominated assets—by some estimates, $22 trillion worth. So while our reserve-currency status may postpone America's day of fiscal reckoning, it could also make that day far more destructive if and when it finally arrives.

The consequences of such a market-driven crisis would extend far beyond Wall Street. Banks would curb consumer and business lending, and the economy would tumble into recession, or even depression. Unemployment would climb as businesses, losing both confidence and customers, cut back on production, lay off workers, and reduce investment in modernization and expansion.

Meanwhile, as tax revenue fell with the shrinking economy, policymakers would be forced to impose draconian spending cuts and tax increases to keep the debt from exploding even more—policy changes that could have devastating effects on our most vulnerable populations. Policymakers might also be forced to pursue policies of "financial repression" such as restricting capital exports or requiring financial institutions and pension plans to hold government debt at levels well above what would be needed for safety and soundness—steps that would penalize the very people we should actually be rewarding, savers.

Despite the false sense of security offered by today's low interest rates, we should remember that markets can and do turn suddenly and surprisingly against debtor nations. Until a few years ago, most governments in the Eurozone could easily borrow money at under 4.5 percent. But then Greece defaulted, and other European Union governments—many experiencing soaring interest rates and sinking credit ratings—struggled to avoid a similar fate. In late 2009, Greek interest rates on ten-year government debt hovered between 4.5 and 5.5 percent. By early 2011, that rate had soared to 12 percent—and by early 2012 was climbing past 25 percent. The attendant economic stagnation that has subsequently afflicted much of the Continent—with persistently low growth and persistently high unemployment, especially among young people—has made it even harder for Europe to take the steps necessary to put its fiscal house in order.

We have also seen that high debt levels can reduce the flexibility of policymakers to respond to such crises. As European nations discovered, when debts are already high, governments have trouble issuing additional debt to stimulate economic growth when a recession hits. A country weighed down by debt often has to suffer passively through a prolonged downturn, as Greece has had to do in recent years. By contrast, a country with a strong fiscal balance sheet can raise funds at reasonable rates and take aggressive action to spur its economy. That's why the United States must take serious steps to address its mounting long-term debt problem before it gets out of hand.

## CLOSING THE BUDGET GAP

At the heart of America's long-term debt challenge is the growing gap between the entitlement benefits we've promised ourselves and how little willingness we've shown to pay for them. That results in a growing mismatch between America's projected tax revenue and its projected spending over the longer term.

Some people believe we should simply cut the spending side alone, to match revenue. This straightforward approach may sound simple and appealing, but it's not politically viable and its fiscal implications would be significant. And while I believe that the solution to reducing long-term debt falls more heavily on the spending side of the ledger, I believe that more revenue—ideally through comprehensive tax reform—must be part of the equation as well.

This is because trying to reduce long-term debt to a sustainable level—and keep it there—through spending cuts alone would require cuts that would be draconian in size. How draconian? Under the CBO's alternative fiscal scenario, we would

# THE GROWING DEBT IS CAUSED BY A STRUCTURAL MISMATCH BETWEEN SPENDING AND REVENUES

**Total Federal Revenue and Spending** (Percentage of GDP)

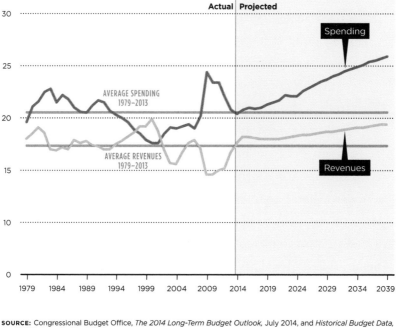

**SOURCE:** Congressional Budget Office, *The 2014 Long-Term Budget Outlook,* July 2014, and *Historical Budget Data,* April 2014. Compiled by PGPF.
**NOTE:** Projections are from CBO's current-law scenario.

have to chop nearly 25 percent of all noninterest federal spending to make our debt sustainable over the next fifty years (by which I mean that our future debt would be no higher than it is today as a share of the economy). And if we were to exclude defense and Social Security from the budget ax, as some suggest, the rest of the budget would have to be cut by 41 percent. I believe cuts of this magnitude would be politically untenable. Moreover, they could eventually sap this nation's ability to invest in its own future, from research to our educational system.

Just as some on the right propose massive and unrealistic spending cuts, some on the left argue that we should address the long-term budget gap only by raising taxes and leaving spending alone. But speaking practically, new taxes alone are not a viable solution to our long-term fiscal problems because to get the job done on their own, such tax increases would have to be so large that they would turn out to be politically untenable and economically counterproductive.

To keep debt no higher than it is today as a share of the economy for the next fifty years through tax increases alone, we'd have to increase overall revenues by more than 30 percent—a hike that I believe would never pass a divided Congress, or a united one. To cover the future costs of Social Security and Medicare simply by raising payroll taxes would require doubling payroll taxes during the lifetime of today's younger workers, which strikes me as economically and politically unthinkable.

For those who wonder if the entire debt problem can be solved by the wealthy, a report from the Tax Policy Center shows that it would be infeasible to stabilize the debt at 60 percent of GDP by raising tax rates on only the top brackets (affecting incomes above $200,000 for married couples)—the top tax rates would have to be more than 90 percent. While I do favor raising revenue from well-off Americans because we can afford more than we're currently paying and because of the disproportionate gains we've had in recent years, tax increases to such an extreme would sap the motivation of some of the most innovative and productive American entrepreneurs, drive investment abroad, and end up undermining the very economic growth that is a key part of solving the long-term debt challenge.

Fortunately, there is a more practical and viable approach to addressing America's long-term debt crisis—using a combination of spending cuts *and* revenue increases. Prominent bipartisan groups, such as Simpson-Bowles and Domenici-Rivlin, have advocated for this approach.

In terms of timing, policy changes should be agreed to now, but should be implemented gradually in order to protect our fragile economic recovery. By announcing future tax increases and benefit cuts in advance, lawmakers could help ease the burden on families by giving them time to adjust their work, saving, and retirement plans. Enacting the reforms now but implementing them later could also provide a much needed boost to business confidence about our fiscal future—and encourage businesses to create jobs and invest in America again.

There are many good ideas for raising revenue that I believe are both fair and economically sound, as I discuss in chapter 6. On the spending side, we should be looking for savings throughout the budget—including defense—as I discuss in chapter 5.

However, it will be virtually impossible to solve the long-term debt problem without also reforming our major entitlement programs for the elderly—Social Security, Medicare, and Medicaid. Together, these entitlements (along with healthcare subsidies) will account for 100 percent of the projected growth in federal spending (apart from interest payments) over the next twenty-five years. The major health programs alone will account for about 70 percent of that increase.

## HEALTHCARE IS THE MAJOR DRIVER OF THE PROJECTED GROWTH IN FEDERAL SPENDING OVER THE LONG TERM

**Federal Spending** (Percentage of GDP)

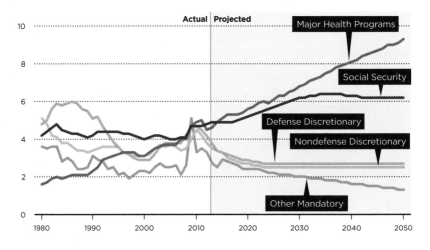

SOURCE: Congressional Budget Office, *Historical Budget Data,* April 2014, and *The 2014 Long-Term Budget Outlook,* July 2014, and PGPF projections based on CBO data. Calculated by PGPF.
NOTE: All projections are based on CBO's current-law scenario. Major health programs include Medicare, Medicaid, Children's Health Insurance Program (CHIP), and the health exchanges.

In coming decades, the costs of these three entitlement programs will be propelled upward by two powerful forces. The first force is the rapid aging of our population. In 2025, the United States will look like a nation of Floridas, with more than one in six Americans aged sixty-five and older. With no offense to Florida (which is a beautiful state whose beaches I have enjoyed visiting), such a demographic distribution will strain budgets because there will be fewer people working to help support a growing population of retirees.

## THE POPULATION OF THE UNITED STATES IS AGING RAPIDLY. SOON WE WILL BE A NATION OF FLORIDAS.

———

**People Age 65 and Older** (Percentage of total population)

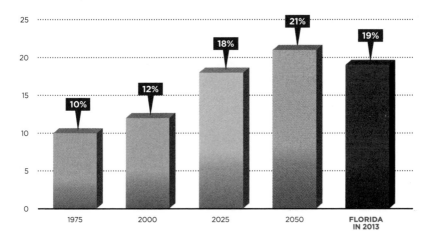

SOURCE: Social Security Administration, *The 2014 Annual Report of the Board of Trustees of the Federal Old-Age and Survivors Insurance and Federal Disability Insurance Trust Funds,* July 2014, and the U.S. Census Bureau. Compiled by PGPF.

The Social Security Administration projects that as the nearly eighty million members of the baby boom generation move into old age, the number of elderly Americans will surge by 75 percent over the next twenty-five years. At the same time, the number of working-age adults available to support those beneficiaries will increase by just 9 percent. In 1970, there were almost four workers for each Social Security beneficiary. The current ratio is about three to one; by 2030, it will only be about two to one.

The second force driving entitlement costs sharply upward, which interacts explosively with the first, is the rapid growth rate of healthcare spending. For example, as longevity continues to increase, Americans eighty-five and older will

## THE AGING OF THE BABY BOOM GENERATION WILL BOOST THE NUMBER OF AMERICANS AGE 65 AND OLDER

**Number of People Age 65 and Older** (Millions)

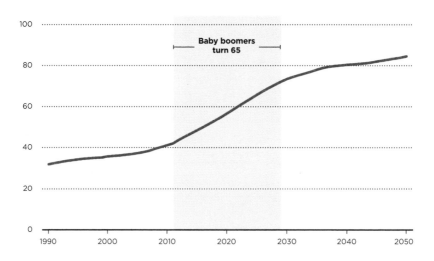

**SOURCE:** U.S. Census Bureau, *Historical National Intercensal Estimates* and *2012 National Population Projections.* Compiled by PGPF.
**NOTE:** The highlighted period represents the time span between the years when the oldest and when the youngest of the baby boom generation turn age 65.

## AS THE POPULATION AGES, FEWER WORKERS WILL BE PAYING TAXES TO SUPPORT EACH SOCIAL SECURITY BENEFICIARY

(Workers per beneficiary)

**SOURCE:** Social Security Administration, *The 2014 Annual Report of the Board of Trustees of the Federal Old-Age and Survivors Insurance and Federal Disability Insurance Trust Funds,* July 2014. Compiled by PGPF.

constitute the fastest-growing segment of the population over the next four decades, and spending on this group is more than five times higher than health spending on adults between nineteen and sixty-four years of age, as illustrated by the following chart. Left unaddressed, these rising costs—multiplied by a rapidly aging population—will have a huge impact on our long-term debt and our economic outlook generally.

## MEDICAL SPENDING INCREASES RAPIDLY WITH AGE

**Annual Health Costs per Person** (Dollars)

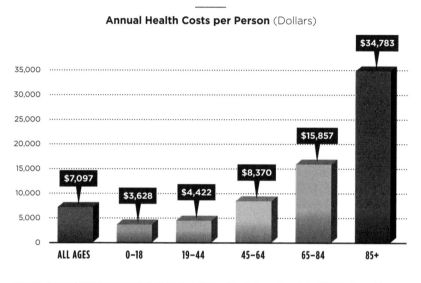

**SOURCE:** Centers for Medicare and Medicaid Services, *National Health Expenditure Data, 2010 Gender and Age Tables*, May 2014. Data are from 2010. Compiled by PGPF.

# A TIME FOR CHOOSING

Can America still avoid this collision with our long-term national debt? The answer is yes, because it is we who are creating this mountain of debt in the first place, and we—through our elected officials—who determine spending and revenue policies. So there is still time to turn the ship, but not if we keep ignoring our own role in its approach. That is, we can't simply hope for another economic boom so big that it will let us grow our way out of the problem. Indeed, the U.S. economy would have to grow about twice as fast as our projected long-term growth rate in every year for twenty-five years to fully fix the fiscal imbalance under the alternative fiscal scenario—a level of economic nirvana we have never recorded in our history. As a result, we have little choice: we simply must rein in the projected growth in long-term debt—but I believe we should do so in a way that protects the most vulnerable.

Many people worry that entitlement reforms would hurt millions of elderly Americans, especially those with low incomes. Such fears might be justified, depending on the approach we take. One approach that is nearly guaranteed to lead to such an outcome is to keep ignoring the reality of mounting long-term debt and permit a financial and economic crisis to develop. Indeed, in a crisis, the politics would probably become brutal as entrenched interests fight over a shrinking economic pie. The safety net could well be shredded, and the vulnerable would likely be the people with the most to lose in a fiscal crisis. Only by tackling the long-term debt challenge soon—and this will necessitate entitlement reform—will we be able to strengthen and sustain the safety net for generations to come.

I believe that protecting the vulnerable is a moral imperative and we must strengthen the social safety net. But the only way to do it is to substantially reduce its overall cost, to make it more sustainable. Indeed, a fiscally sustainable safety net is ultimately the only way to ensure that benefits for vulnerable Americans will be there when they are most needed.

# 3

## STRENGTHENING AND SUSTAINING SOCIAL SECURITY FOR GENERATIONS TO COME

E nacted during the Great Depression as a bulwark against poverty in old age, Social Security remains a central pillar of America's social compact. As a matter of principle, our society has long believed that senior citizens deserve the dignity of basic economic security in retirement. This was true when President Franklin Delano Roosevelt signed Social Security into law in 1935, and it remains true today. That's why we must address the fiscal challenges of this fundamental entitlement sooner rather than later, so that we can strengthen and sustain Social Security for generations to come—particularly for the most vulnerable. Social Security isn't just mandatory by law; it's also a moral imperative under our society.

That said, demographic changes and fiscal realities will present America with a serious challenge in decades to come:

how to meet our nation's rapidly growing Social Security obligations. To be sure, Social Security is not as troubled financially as our healthcare programs are. As discussed in chapter 2, the growth in federal spending over the long term is projected to arise solely from increases in spending on Social Security, major health programs, and interest on the debt. Social Security accounts for only 30 percent of the growth of noninterest spending, while the health programs account for the remaining 70 percent.

But because Social Security plays such a critical role in many people's retirement, it is critically important to put the pro-

## LOW-INCOME SENIORS RELY ON SOCIAL SECURITY BENEFITS FOR A MAJOR SHARE OF THEIR RETIREMENT INCOME

**Social Security Benefits** (Percentage of total income)

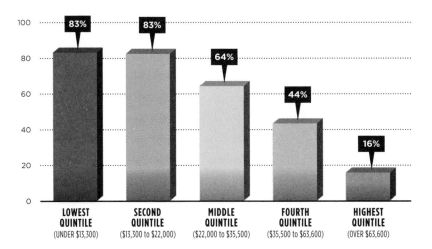

SOURCE: Social Security Administration, *Income of the Population 55 or Older, 2012,* April 2014. Compiled by PGPF.
NOTE: A quintile is one fifth of the distribution. The lowest quintile is the 20% of the 65+ population with the lowest income.

gram on a sustainable footing. Social Security provides more than 80 percent of the monthly income for seniors in the bottom two quintiles of income.

Consider the scope of the financial challenges facing Social Security. As the following chart illustrates, the Social Security program, which is already in cash deficit, will face growing deficits in coming decades as a result of a demographic trends that create a growing mismatch between scheduled benefits and revenues (which are largely Social Security payroll taxes).

Social Security started running annual cash deficits in 2010. Cumulatively, the federal government is projected to borrow $2.8 trillion to cover the program's deficits between 2013 (the last year of actual data in the latest projection from the Social Security trustees) and 2033, when the trust fund will become, by the trustees' own definition, insolvent. When that happens, according to the 2014 Social Security trustees' report, benefits would have to be cut 23 percent in one fell swoop—unless Congress and the president take action before then to pass significant reforms.

Some insist that Social Security does not add to our current budget deficit and argue that Social Security should therefore be exempt from any significant reform. But the reality is that Social Security is already adding to today's budget deficit because, as we have just discussed, it is paying out billions more in benefits than it is taking in. Social Security did collect more in payroll taxes and other revenues than it spent in benefits from 1984 to 2009. However, for the government as a whole, those surpluses were not saved but spent, and were simply ex-

# SOCIAL SECURITY MOVED FROM ANNUAL SURPLUSES TO ANNUAL DEFICITS IN 2010

Social Security Surpluses/Deficits (Percentage of GDP)

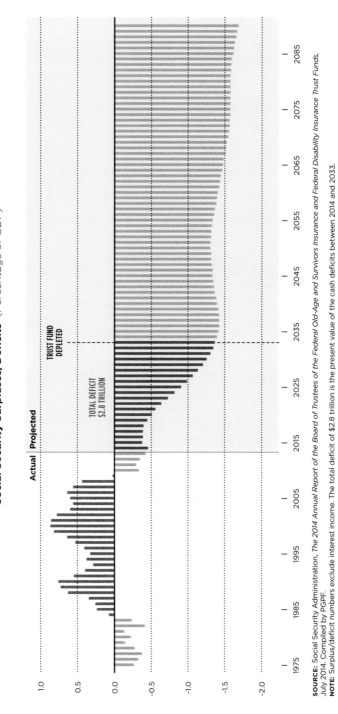

TRUST FUND DEPLETED

TOTAL DEFICIT $2.8 TRILLION

Actual | Projected

SOURCE: Social Security Administration, *The 2014 Annual Report of the Board of Trustees of the Federal Old-Age and Survivors Insurance and Federal Disability Insurance Trust Funds*, July 2014. Compiled by PGPF.
NOTE: Surplus/deficit numbers exclude interest income. The total deficit of $2.8 trillion is the present value of the cash deficits between 2014 and 2033.

changed for a stack of IOUs that the government has written to itself—making the term "Social Security trust fund" an accounting oxymoron.

To help understand the true state of the trust fund, consider an alternative scenario where the trust fund didn't exist. What would be different about federal spending, revenues, and deficits over the next twenty years? Absolutely nothing. The federal government would still have to borrow the same amount of money as it does now to make up the difference between the Social Security revenue coming in (mainly from Social Security payroll taxes) and the larger benefits flowing out.

## BALANCING BENEFITS AND BURDENS

Some argue that if Social Security benefits were reduced for better-off Americans, political support for this important program would erode. This concept is captured in the old cliché "Programs for the poor are poor programs." But Social Security is not a program intended only for the poor, and I do not believe that reforms should transform it into a program only for the poor—lowering benefits for the wealthy does not do so. Making Social Security financially sustainable is really the only way to ensure that benefits for vulnerable Americans will be there when they are needed.

I believe that most Americans would understand the basic math and the moral imperative to help those who need it most. Thus, there is the fundamental question of whether, with budgets strained and resources limited, and with the population rapidly aging, we should be providing the full roster of benefits (including Social Security) to those of us who don't actually need them. To me, the answer is obviously no. In all our benefit programs, I believe we must ensure that reforms protect the poor and vulnerable.

We should also consider delaying the implementation of changes in Social Security benefits in order to give people still in the workforce time to prepare. For instance, many Social Security reform proposals do not affect people who are aged fifty-five or older. I also personally believe that new revenue should be part of the solution for Social Security, but we also need to adjust benefits. This will involve difficult trade-offs, courageous political decisions, and, inevitably, some trial and error.

## OPTIONS FOR REFORM

Fortunately, there are many ways to reduce Social Security's overall budgetary burden without risking the safety net that it provides for the vulnerable. Progressive price indexing (sometimes called progressive wage indexing) is one such reform. Under the current rules, a retiree's initial Social Security benefits are determined by a formula associated with overall wage growth, which typically rises faster than inflation.

Progressive price indexing would change the index used to calculate first-year benefits for higher-earning retirees. The new indexing would reduce those retirees' benefits, but the reductions would be phased in gradually over time, so that workers would have ample time to prepare for the new system. It could be designed so that workers within ten years of retirement would see no changes in their benefits and, for lower-income earners, the current system would remain in place no matter when they retired.

Many experts also recommend changing the index used to adjust benefits for inflation each year after the first-year benefits are set. The Consumer Price Index (CPI), currently used to calculate inflation, also forms the basis for Social Security's annual cost of living adjustments (COLAs). Many economists believe the CPI, as currently calculated, overstates the actual inflation rate. As a result, Social Security benefits rise more than actual inflation. If a more accurate CPI measure were used for adjusting benefits (such as the "chained CPI"), the federal government could slow the growth of Social Security's costs while sufficiently preserving the purpose of adjusting benefits in the first place, which is to protect retirees from inflation.

Of course, if Social Security benefits were adjusted using a better measure of inflation, the same measure should be used to adjust the parameters of the tax code that are also increased for inflation each year. In particular, CPI is currently used to make annual inflation adjustments in the income tax brackets, the personal exemption, and some other provisions in the tax code. Using a more accurate measure of inflation would result in more people in higher tax brackets over time and would thus generate more revenue.

Another reform that's often suggested as a way to lower costs is raising the Social Security retirement age. Proponents argue that raising the age at which Americans can begin collecting Social Security benefits makes sense because people are living substantially longer than they were when Social Security was first enacted. In 1940, men who reached sixty-five years old were expected to live, on average, to be about seventy-seven or seventy-eight. Today, the average sixty-five-year-old man is expected to live to be eighty-four. This increase of six or seven years may not seem dramatic, but when combined with a surge in the number of Americans who will be retiring over coming decades, the resulting stress on the Social Security system will be substantial.

However, as the following chart indicates, it is important to recognize that longevity increases have been far greater for people who earn higher incomes during their working years.

Today, men at age sixty-five whose earnings are below the national median have a life expectancy more than five years shorter than those above the national median. As a result, proposals to raise the Social Security retirement age could end up hurting lower-income retirees more than higher-income retirees—an important factor to consider in determining how to reform the system.

Another factor to consider (and an ethically and logistically complicated one) is how to account for the different demands that physical and white-collar jobs make on those who do them. In other words, it may be relatively painless to raise the retirement age for a business executive, but what about for an older worker doing hard physical labor? All work, at any age, is hardly equal.

## INCREASES IN LONGEVITY HAVE BEEN GREATER FOR HIGHER EARNERS

### Life Expectancy of a Male 65-Year-Old

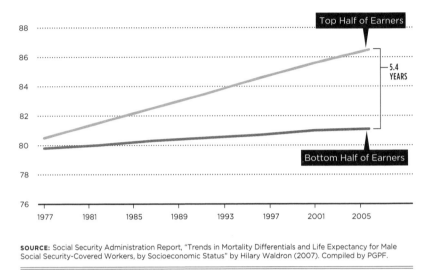

SOURCE: Social Security Administration Report, "Trends in Mortality Differentials and Life Expectancy for Male Social Security-Covered Workers, by Socioeconomic Status" by Hilary Waldron (2007). Compiled by PGPF.

If raising the retirement age proves to be a point on which all sides can agree, it will be necessary to protect those at the lower end of the income scale, perhaps by increasing their benefits. Also, Social Security beneficiaries should be given time to prepare for any change to the retirement age. Given this, these changes would have to be phased in over time, so as not to affect those who are already near retirement.

On the revenue side, a widely discussed option is to raise the cap on the share of income subject to payroll taxes. It's a progressive reform that would cost more for people whose income is above the payroll tax cutoff point ($117,000 in 2014), but cost nothing for those under the current cap.

Another potential revenue raiser is changing the taxation of Social Security benefits for high-income seniors. Currently, no one pays income tax on more than 85 percent of his or her Social Security benefits. This cap could be lifted so that 100 percent of benefits are taxable for high-income retirees.

## IMPROVING RETIREMENT SECURITY

Americans currently save too little for their retirement. In 2013, according to the Federal Reserve, half of American families did not have a retirement account, such as a 401(k) or IRA, and presumably had no or very limited retirement savings. Among those with a retirement account, the median amount saved was just $59,000—far from adequate to enjoy a secure retirement, let alone a comfortable one.

One way to address these problems of savings adequacy is to introduce mandatory personal retirement savings accounts to supplement Social Security. These "add-on" accounts would be funded through additional contributions from workers. To ease the burden on low-income workers, contributions from those workers could be supplemented with government subsidies. Add-on accounts could increase total savings in the economy—something we desperately need. To avoid giving Washington another cookie jar, these savings would remain under the control of the private citizens. Individuals would fully own their retirement savings accounts and could make decisions about how to invest them, as members of Congress currently do with their savings accounts through the federal government's Thrift Savings Plan. The accounts would have to be designed so that their owners could only tap into them upon retirement or for other restricted purposes, such as medical expenses. Otherwise, the effect on national saving could be significantly diminished.

## THE NEED TO REFORM SOCIAL SECURITY NOW

There is an important final reason to promote Social Security reform now: it is technically the easiest entitlement to fix. The options are well known and well understood. While the politics may be complicated, the math isn't. Improving Social Security's finances is a relatively straightforward matter of adjusting the formulas for benefits and taxes. Ultimately, we need our political leaders to reach the compromises needed to strengthen Social Security for those who rely on it most, and do so in a fair and fiscally responsible manner.

# 4

# PATH TO HEALTH

Reforming U.S. Healthcare to Save
Lives, Money, and Our Future

I n a 2013 investigative article that captured the anomalies of
U.S. healthcare, the *New York Times* told the story of an
American named Michael Shopenn, who—suffering from
severe, chronic pain from arthritis—flew to Belgium to have
his hip replaced. He went there because Belgian doctors
quoted a price that was—for the same operation, using the
same American-made artificial hip—at least $65,000 less than
the price for the same operation in America. The surgery
transformed Shopenn's life, and he is now back to his active
lifestyle.

If only the American healthcare system were so healthy. Unfortunately, it's not. And Shopenn's case is just one example of
a broader epidemic—runaway U.S. healthcare costs.

# THE ECONOMIC COSTS OF AN AILING HEALTHCARE SECTOR

By all accounts, U.S. healthcare spending is already inordinately high and will continue rising in the future, threatening not just the federal budget, but our ability to remain a competitive and growing economy—to say nothing of the costs it imposes on family and business budgets. Our health spending per person is more than twice the average of other advanced nations in the OECD, and over the past thirty years, healthcare spending has doubled relative to the size of our economy.

Yet despite this high level of spending, our overall health outcomes are generally no better, and sometimes worse, than other nations. Compared with other countries, we rank in the middle of the pack in terms of heart attack fatalities and complications during surgery—and near the bottom of the pack in terms of hospital admissions for unmanaged asthma and infant mortality. Indeed, our infant mortality rate ranks thirty-first among the OECD's thirty-four nations—only Turkey, Mexico, and Chile have higher rates. Moreover, our infant mortality rates are particularly high among poor and minority populations.

According to the Institute of Medicine (IOM), as much as 30 percent of total healthcare expenditures goes to care that adds little or no value. The IOM also finds that it takes the U.S. healthcare industry seventeen years to adopt a cost-effective innovation.

# AMERICANS SPEND MORE THAN TWICE AS MUCH PER CAPITA ON HEALTHCARE AS THE AVERAGE DEVELOPED COUNTRY DOES

## Per Capita Healthcare Costs (Dollars)

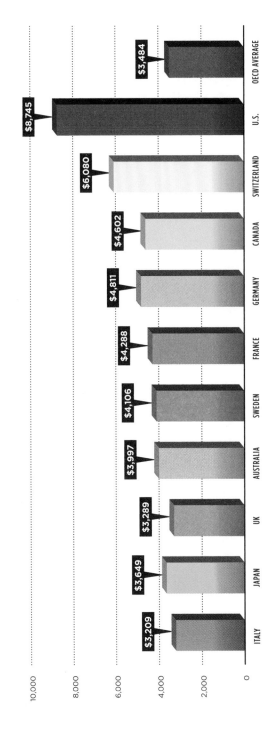

| Country | Cost |
|---|---|
| ITALY | $3,209 |
| JAPAN | $3,649 |
| UK | $3,289 |
| AUSTRALIA | $3,997 |
| SWEDEN | $4,106 |
| FRANCE | $4,288 |
| GERMANY | $4,811 |
| CANADA | $4,602 |
| SWITZERLAND | $6,080 |
| U.S. | $8,745 |
| OECD AVERAGE | $3,484 |

**SOURCE:** Organization for Economic Cooperation and Development, *OECD Health Statistics 2014*, June 2014. Compiled by PGPF.
**NOTE:** Per capita health expenditures are for the year 2012, except Australia, for which 2011 data are the latest available. Chart uses purchasing power parities to convert data into dollars.

## ALTHOUGH THE UNITED STATES SPENDS MORE ON HEALTHCARE THAN OTHER DEVELOPED COUNTRIES, ITS HEALTH OUTCOMES ARE GENERALLY NO BETTER

Worst ← —————————————————— → Best

**Unmanaged Asthma**
Avoidable hospital admissions
U.S.
SLOVAK REPUBLIC · · · · · · · · · · · · · · · · · · ITALY

**Unmanaged Diabetes**
Avoidable hospital admissions
U.S.
HUNGARY · · · · · · · · · · · · · · · · ITALY

**Patient Safety During Childbirth**
Obstetric trauma rates
U.S.
DENMARK · · · · · · · · · · · · · POLAND

**Surgical Complications**
Foreign body left in during procedure
U.S.
SWITZERLAND · · · · · · · · · · BELGIUM

**Heart Attack Mortality**
Age-standardized rates
U.S.
SLOVAK REPUBLIC · · · · · · · · · · · · · · · JAPAN

**Infant Mortality**
U.S.
MEXICO · · · · · · · · · · · · · · · · · ICELAND

**Life Expectancy at Birth**
U.S.
MEXICO · · · · · · · · · · · · · · · · · SWITZERLAND

**Patient Satisfaction**
Percentage who feel that doctor spends enough time with patient in consultation
U.S.
SWEDEN · · · · · · · · · CZECH REPUBLIC

**SOURCE:** Organization for Economic Cooperation and Development, *Health at a Glance 2013: OECD Indicators.* Compiled by PGPF.
**NOTE:** Data are not available for all countries for all metrics; all published OECD data are shown. Data are for 2011 or latest available.

Although the growth of national health spending has slowed recently, it is still projected to climb in the years ahead, according to the Congressional Budget Office. Within twenty-five years, the CBO projects that healthcare consumption by both the private and public sectors will reach 22 percent of

GDP, up from 16 percent in 2012. To be sure, all projections about the future are uncertain. But uncertainty about future growth of healthcare costs is not a valid argument for delaying reform. To the contrary, uncertainty is actually an argument for doing more to solve the problem of rising healthcare costs. As I mentioned in chapter 2, people address uncertainty about the future in their personal lives by setting aside some extra money for a "rainy day"—that is, they hedge that risk by taking action in advance. Similarly, if governments are uncertain

## TOTAL U.S. HEALTH EXPENDITURES (BOTH PUBLIC AND PRIVATE) ARE PROJECTED TO RISE TO NEARLY ONE-QUARTER OF THE ECONOMY BY 2039

**National Health Spending** (Percentage of GDP)

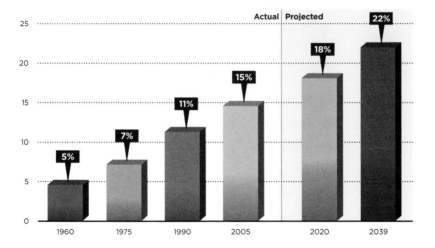

SOURCE: Centers for Medicare and Medicaid Services, *National Health Expenditures,* September 2013 and January 2014; and the Congressional Budget Office, *The 2014 Long-Term Budget Outlook,* July 2014. Compiled by PGPF.
NOTE: CMS data used for years 1960–2020. The 2039 figure reflects the latest projection from CBO. National spending on healthcare is health consumption expenditures as defined in the national health expenditure accounts and excludes spending on medical research, structures, and equipment.

## BETWEEN 1999 AND 2039, SPENDING ON FEDERAL HEALTH PROGRAMS IS PROJECTED TO DOUBLE

**Federal Spending** (Percentage of GDP)

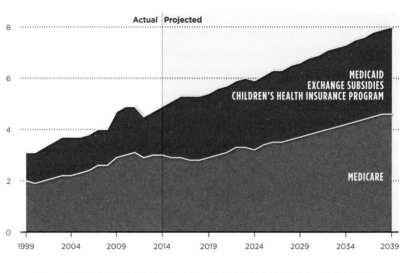

SOURCE: Congressional Budget Office, *The 2014 Long-Term Budget Outlook,* July 2014. Compiled by PGPF.
NOTE: All projections are from CBO's current-law scenario.

about future healthcare costs, they should be hedging that risk by adopting policies to reduce costs.

Growing healthcare costs will put huge strains on the federal budget, especially as members of the large baby boom generation reach age sixty-five and become eligible for Medicare and, for those seniors with low incomes, Medicaid. Indeed, the interaction between aging and health costs has a powerful effect on the federal budget. Not surprisingly, the share of the budget (excluding interest) devoted to the federal government's major health programs will soar from 26 percent in 2014 to almost 40 percent within twenty-five years. Moreover, those major health programs are projected to account for about 70 percent of the increase in noninterest spending over the long run.

Spending so much of our national income on healthcare undermines our economy in many ways. It means our nation has far less income for saving and investing in other areas; nonhealth businesses have fewer resources to expand and create jobs; cash wages stagnate or decline; and there are many fewer resources for the country to devote to critically needed investments to enhance America's current and future competitiveness. The benefits of controlling runaway healthcare costs are immense: at the personal level, if we brought today's health spending in line with that of other countries, a family of four, on average, could have an extra $14,000 a year to spend, save, and invest; or we could provide enormous resources for making critically needed public investments in our economic future.

## THE NEED FOR
## FUNDAMENTAL CHANGE

The debate over the cost of healthcare often obscures an essential truth: we can only make healthcare more affordable for governments, businesses, families, and individuals by fundamentally changing the way it is delivered, received, and paid for. These underlying changes will necessitate far more than just nibbling around the edges of one or two parts of the healthcare system;

it will require finding ways to increase value throughout the entire chain of prevention, diagnosis, treatment, and recovery.

Some people may find the concept of "value" off-putting when it comes to healthcare—they may associate the word with cheapness, or lower quality. But increasing healthcare value should be about getting equal or better care for fewer dollars. Such a goal is, in fact, achievable given the massive inefficiencies in the current system.

As evidence of those massive inefficiencies, consider the extraordinary and inexplicable variations in healthcare procedures and costs around the country, even when costs are adjusted for different demographics and local living costs. According to scholars at the Dartmouth Institute for Health Policy and Clinical Practice, Medicare recipients in some parts of the United States have seven times more back operations and fifteen times more prostate screenings than in others. Women over sixty-five in Grand Forks, North Dakota, are seven times more likely to have a mastectomy for early-stage breast cancer than women in San Francisco. Similarly, the rate of shoulder replacement is ten times higher in Provo, Utah, than in Syracuse, New York.

Regional variations in prices are just as shocking. A 2013 study found that when 122 hospitals were asked how much they would charge for hip-replacement surgery, the list price varied from $11,100 to $125,798.* The National Commission on Physician

---

*Jaime Rosenthal, Xin Lu, and Peter Cram, "Availability of Consumer Prices from US Hospitals for a Common Surgical Procedure," *JAMA Internal Medicine* 173, no. 6 (March 2013): 427–32.

Payment Reform found that Medicare pays more for procedures done in hospitals than when those same procedures are performed in doctors' offices. An echocardiogram done in a hospital costs Medicare $450, while the same procedure costs $180 in a physician's office, according to former Senate majority leader Bill Frist and Dr. Steven Schroeder, cochairs of the commission.

To me, these symptoms suggest fundamental flaws in the way our healthcare sector operates. In my wide array of experience in industry, government, and the nonprofit sector, I have never seen such huge and inexplicable variations in costs. Such waste and inefficiency would not be tolerated in other major American sectors, where there is more of a laserlike focus on value, outcomes, and implementing best practices.


## DIAGNOSING FACTORS EXPLAINING HIGH HEALTHCARE COSTS

Several factors can explain the high current costs in our system.


### *Fee-For-Service and Third-Party Payment*

Perhaps the most fundamental issue is our fee-for-service system. Under fee-for-service, we pay for the volume of healthcare services delivered, not for the value of those services or the outcomes they achieve. So when providers perform more procedures (regardless of the procedures' usefulness), their income increases. Those higher costs are then passed on to insurers, who in turn pass them on to policyholders, the government, or other payers.

Because the link between who uses healthcare and who pays for it is indirect, the normal brakes that control costs in other markets don't work well in the healthcare market. As a result, providers don't need to pay much attention to costs and often gravitate toward the newest and often most expensive treatments, drugs, and devices. Meanwhile, most patients are largely insulated from the cost of their care. Their insurance company (or the government) usually pays most of the bill.

## THE UNITED STATES PERFORMS A HIGH NUMBER OF MRI EXAMS COMPARED WITH OTHER COUNTRIES

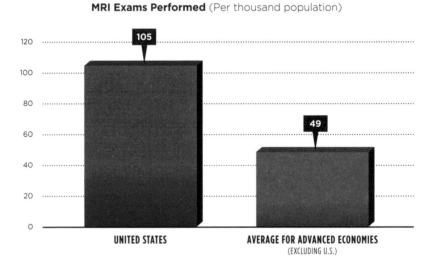

**MRI Exams Performed** (Per thousand population)

**SOURCE:** Organization for Economic Cooperation and Development, *OECD Health Statistics 2014,* June 2014. Compiled by PGPF.
**NOTE:** U.S. data are from 2012 and the average for advanced economies are from 2012 or the latest data available.

In fact, consumers' out-of-pocket costs have declined sharply as a share of total health spending (private plus public payments). In 1970, out-of-pocket costs financed 33 percent of total health spending. But by 2012, they covered only 12 percent of total costs.

Similarly, employees are also generally unaware of the true cost of their insurance. In many cases, their employers pick up

## CONSUMER OUT-OF-POCKET SPENDING IS DECLINING AS A SHARE OF NATIONAL HEALTH SPENDING

**Source of Payment** (Percentage of national health expenditures)

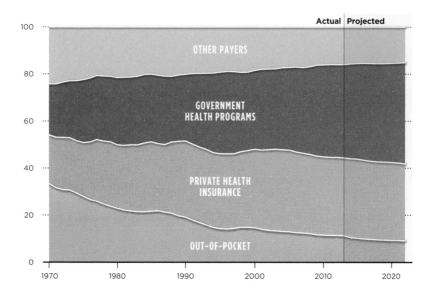

**SOURCE:** Centers for Medicare and Medicaid, *National Health Expenditures,* January 2013. Compiled by PGPF.
**NOTE:** Government health programs include Medicare, Medicaid, CHIP, and the health programs of the Department of Defense and the Department of Veterans Affairs. CMS defines "out-of-pocket spending" as direct spending by consumers for all healthcare goods and services not covered by insurance and includes coinsurance and deductibles. Premiums paid by individuals for private health insurance are counted as part of private health insurance.

most of the costs. And although employers eventually shift most of those costs back to workers in the form of lower wages, those shifts occur slowly—and often imperceptibly—over time. So most workers are unaware of how much rising healthcare costs have slowed the growth of their real wages over time.

## Tax Subsidies for Employer-Provided Health Insurance

Awareness about the true cost of employer-provided insurance is further dulled by our tax system, which subsidizes it to the tune of about $300 billion per year. Currently, healthcare benefits are not taxable for employees who receive them from their employer, and companies can deduct their cost of providing insurance as a business expense.

## Delegated Decision Making

With virtually no knowledge of how much healthcare costs and little reason to care, patients do not have the incentive to keep costs down. Moreover, because consumers rely so heavily on the advice of their doctors, they effectively delegate decision-making authority to providers who, as I mentioned earlier, have a financial incentive to do more rather than less.

## Technology

Many point to technology as another key factor driving increased costs. This may seem puzzling—in most sectors of the economy, innovations in technology drive down costs. But in healthcare, technology and innovation drive our spending higher and higher. While sometimes innovations lead to improved outcomes, new technologies often result in health outcomes that are no better than the results achieved by the existing approaches that they seek to replace and could, in a few cases, even be harmful. In other cases, the health benefits may exist, but may be marginal and not worth the added cost.

So why does technology *increase* costs in the medical sector while it *decreases* costs in other sectors? There are many reasons, which were explored in a recent RAND study, "Redirecting Innovation in U.S. Health Care," funded by the Gates Foundation. In America's healthcare system, providers and consumers pay little attention to price because of the widespread use of insurance, the prevalence of fee-for-service reimbursements, and the lack of price transparency. This general price insensitivity signals to the market that price is not an issue—when an innovation is approved, demand will be there regardless of cost. This drives research and investment toward costly technologies, so innovators are incented to invest in solutions with high revenue opportunity, even if the health benefit is marginal. Conversely, there is less incentive for innovators to develop cost-reducing technologies. When fee-for-service insurance covers the costs, neither patients nor providers see much financial gain from using lower-cost technology, so the demand for (and revenue opportunity from) these types of innovations is limited. In addition, key stakeholders are not well positioned to reap the benefits of a cost-reducing innovation because they often interact with patients for only limited periods of time and because the delivery of care is highly fragmented. Further, as a society, we place a high value on inventing drugs, medical devices, and diagnostic tools that expand our scientific capability to extend life, regardless of the cost. And in many cases, these innovations cost more in the United States than they do in other nations.

## Multiple Chronic Conditions

Although the lack of consumer cost consciousness is an important driver of healthcare costs, the problems with our health-

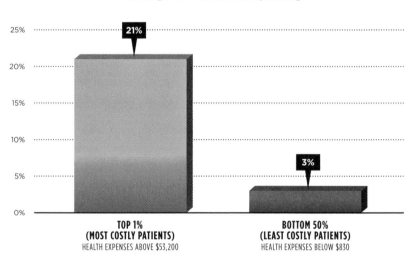

**ANNUAL HEALTHCARE SPENDING IS CONCENTRATED ON A SMALL PORTION OF THE OVERALL POPULATION**

Percentage of Total Health Spending

SOURCE: Kaiser Family Foundation, *Concentration of Health Care Spending in the U.S. Population, 2010*, March 2013. Compiled by PGPF.

## ONE IN FOUR MEDICARE DOLLARS IS SPENT ON PEOPLE WHO ARE IN THE LAST YEAR OF LIFE

**25%**
Medicare Spending in the Last Year of Life

**75%**
Other Medicare Spending

SOURCE: Health Services Research, *Long-Term Trends in Medicare Payments in the Last Year of Life,* April 2010. Compiled by PGPF.
NOTE: Data are from 2006, the most recent available.

care market cannot be solved simply by making patients more aware of the costs of their treatments. As we search for ways to drive greater efficiency in healthcare delivery, we must focus on where the money is spent. Indeed, one of the most stunning statistics about our healthcare system is that 5 percent of the U.S. population—mainly those who suffer from multiple chronic conditions—accounts for 50 percent of the nation's health expenditures. Similarly, spending devoted to care during the last year of life accounts for about 25 percent of Medicare expenditures. So any effective improvements to delivery and value in these areas will contribute greatly to controlling overall healthcare spending while also providing patients with better results.

## Fragmentation

These problems are exacerbated by fragmentation within our healthcare delivery system. Too often, our health providers work independently of each other and do not collaborate or coordinate. This fragmentation reduces the quality of care (especially for patients with multiple chronic conditions), results in repetitive tests, and leads to excessive administrative costs. According to the IOM, the U.S. healthcare system spent $190 billion on excess administrative costs in 2009. No doubt, we have all experienced the frustration of filling out very similar (but not identical) forms on every visit to the doctor, taking up time and requiring more office staff to process all the paperwork.

## Lack of Information

Fragmentation in the healthcare system and the lack of integrated medical care also make it difficult to develop consistent and usable data on cost, quality, and patient experience. While there is no shortage of raw data in our healthcare system, by and large, such information is scattered, buried, fragmented, not comparable, and difficult to access and use. These data are essential for finding ways to improve the quality of U.S. healthcare, reducing its costs, and minimizing the inexplicable variation in costs I mentioned earlier about which little has been done.

## Medical Liability

The lack of consensus on the effectiveness and appropriateness of treatments also makes it more difficult to develop a clear set of standards for defining what would be considered "good medical practice." Without the benefit of a clear set of standards, many medical doctors may feel that it is necessary to perform extra tests and procedures with only marginal benefits because they are afraid of being sued for malpractice. By some estimates, medical liability (including so-called defensive medicine) costs us about $55 billion a year.

## No Global Budget

Finally, unlike other developed countries, the United States does not have a fixed overall budget for federal health spending. While I don't claim that a firm budget would always keep costs under control, America's current "open wallet" approach likely contributes to higher prices and an increase in the number of medical procedures performed, relative to other advanced economies.

The reader may note that I say very little about the Affordable Care Act (ACA or "Obamacare"). The reason is that the primary objective of the Act is not to address the issue of this chapter—the critical economic and fiscal challenge of America's inefficient healthcare system. To be fair, the ACA has taken steps toward controlling health costs by changing the tax treatment of "Cadillac health plans" and enacting other measures, such as piloting bundled payment programs that could reduce costs while maintaining the quality of care. But in my opinion, the legislation did not go far enough to address many of the fundamental drivers of healthcare cost growth, including the predominance of fee-for-service reimbursement.

# TREATMENTS FOR
# THE HEALTHCARE SECTOR

To move us in the right direction, we need to undertake a number of initiatives that can transform the way that healthcare is delivered, received, and paid for in our country. Those reforms should include both positive and negative financial incentives to encourage doctors and hospitals to coordinate their efforts and focus more on care quality and cost, not volume and income. We need to encourage disruptive innovations that make the health market more like other markets where providers compete to create value for consumers and where technology is cost decreasing not cost increasing. And we need to increase cost consciousness throughout the entire health system, from providers to payers to employers to patients. That means involving all groups, including physicians, health professionals, drug companies, and other medical suppliers; health plans and insurance companies; employers and workers; government; and consumers.

There are a number of promising initiatives for reforming our health delivery system:

## Moving Away from Fee-for-Service

There are several innovative approaches for moving away from fee-for-service that could reduce costs while improving the quality of care. One approach is to expand the use of "capitated payments," which give providers a fixed monthly amount for each patient (adjusted for that patient's health status and risk of illness) for a specific set of health services.

This approach could be combined with a greater use of incentives. For example, we could provide bonuses for those who achieve higher quality at lower cost—and publicize the methods that work best. Medicare now has the ability to reduce payments to certain hospitals that fail to lower their rates of preventable readmissions, and does not pay for hospital-acquired infections. We could build on this progress by expanding penalties for doctors and hospitals whose patients have unnecessarily high rates of readmission to the hospital, acquire hospital-based infections, or suffer as a result of avoidable medical errors.

## Enhancing Coordinated Care

We also need to find ways to shift our entire healthcare system toward integrated care. Many Americans have experienced a sense of disquiet (or worse) when it becomes apparent that many of their caregivers don't know what treatments the others on their case are using. Not only would better coordination improve patient care, but it would also reduce unnecessary duplication of services and avoid potentially harmful drug interactions.

## *Integrated Care*

There are a number of successful models of health providers that offer integrated, coordinated care. For example, the Geisinger Health System, the Cleveland Clinic, and the Mayo Clinic have been able to provide outstanding value in health-care compared with other providers. We need to develop more incentives to motivate providers to set up more of these kinds of systems that integrate providers (from primary care through post-acute care) into seamless delivery networks.

## *Medical Homes*

So-called medical homes are another example of an innovative approach. These organizations treat the "whole patient," and coordinate care across multiple providers. Because the medical homes are explicitly designed to facilitate coordinated care, they are more likely to take the time to manage care holistically, which can improve health outcomes at lower cost, especially for patients with many chronic conditions. In some instances, medical homes have encouraged more nonphysicians, such as nurse practitioners and physician assistants, to practice "at the top of their license," which allows doctors to focus on more complicated cases and procedures. However, more innovation and further development will be required before these homes can realize their full potential for improving value in acute and long-term care.

## Management of Chronic Illness

A for-profit Medicare Advantage plan, CareMore is another model that is worth studying. It has developed an intensive management model for the frail and chronically ill patients who constitute about 20 percent of their members and 60 percent of their medical costs. Notably, CareMore achieves better-than-average health outcomes while making a profit. For example, according to the *Atlantic* magazine, CareMore's hospitalization rate is 24 percent below the national average; hospital stays are 38 percent shorter; and the amputation rate among diabetics is 60 percent lower than average. How? Care-More invests in patient interventions, such as wireless scales to monitor patient weight and case management that helps save money by reducing costly hospitalizations.

## Accountable Care Organizations (ACOs)

ACOs offer another promising approach for coordinating care. They organize multiple providers—general practitioners, specialists, hospitals, and post-acute care facilities—into highly coordinated groups. Risk-based ACOs are responsible for taking care of a group of patients for a monthly per-patient payment. If they are able to deliver care that meets an acceptable level of quality at a lower cost, the ACO gains. But if their costs are higher, they have to absorb the overage. This approach thus creates incentives for providers to change how care is delivered, so that it lowers costs but maintains quality.

## Expanding Bundled Payments

Bundled payments offer another innovative way of compensating providers by focusing on "episodes of care." Instead of paying doctors and hospitals for conducting tests, filling hospital beds, office visits, and delivering other services, this approach gives providers one payment to cover all costs for an episode of care, such as for a hip fracture or stroke.

Because bundled payments remove the perverse incentive to provide excessive care in order to reap higher payments, they can help focus providers on improving the efficiency and effectiveness of the care they deliver. Indeed, the evidence is still preliminary, but is promising: a recent review of more than fifty studies by the Agency for Healthcare Research and Quality estimated that transitioning from fee-for-service reimbursement to bundled payments could lead to spending reductions of up to 10 percent.

However, additional innovation is needed in this area. For bundled payments to be truly transformative, they will need to coordinate care across organizational boundaries. To accomplish that goal successfully, the organizations will need to integrate their information technology (IT) systems. So far, that IT infrastructure has been slow to develop.

## Promoting Better Access to Data on Costs, Quality, and Effectiveness

We should promote greater access to cost and clinical data to develop better performance metrics and improve accountability throughout the healthcare system. This will encourage more informed decision making about what care should be provided and how much it should cost. Those data are essential for enabling the healthcare system to operate more like a rational market. Such comparative information is virtually impossible to obtain today in any systematic way.

With such information, we would be in a much better position to develop and communicate "best practices" in healthcare delivery and then provide payment incentives for doctors and patients to adhere to these best practices.

Promulgation of care guidelines based on clinical evidence and best practices could also help reduce the costs of defensive medicine. Physicians who could prove that they followed those guidelines could be given "safe harbor" protection from lawsuits, which would reduce the excessive and wasteful defensive care that physicians too often deliver today.

To be sure, there are many good ideas that hold the promise of further quality improvements and cost savings, but which still need more time and evidence to demonstrate their value. Before these ideas are put into widespread practice, we may need additional pilot studies to assess these new approaches and validate their effectiveness.

# REFORMING MEDICARE
# AND MEDICAID

Our ability to effectively reform the way healthcare is delivered and paid for in America will have a profound effect on the federal budget. Most of the factors that drive costs in the overall health sector also drive costs in the federal health programs, but there are some unique aspects of those federal programs that limit the government's ability to control costs.

Medicare, for example, does not use its market power to purchase drugs at lower costs on behalf of seniors. Yet studies indicate that Medicare could reduce its prescription drug spending—which accounted for about 13 percent of Medicare costs in 2013—by consolidating drug purchases and using the huge size of the Medicare population to bargain for lower drug prices.

Medicare generally does not target its payments toward care that is more cost effective. When Medicare does attempt to save money, it tends to simply pay less for procedures. While this can lead to some cost cutting, it also causes doctors and hospitals to shift costs from the government to other payers, or simply increase the volume of services they deliver, to make up for a shortfall in revenue. The net result reduces the savings in *overall* healthcare costs.

The Affordable Care Act created a new fifteen-member board (called the Independent Payment Advisory Board, or IPAB) to focus on containing the growth of Medicare costs. But its powers are limited and, so far, no one has been nominated to serve on it. By statute, it cannot propose increasing Medicare premiums, reducing benefit coverage, changing benefits, or rationing care. Although the IPAB has the power to recommend cost containment measures that would go into effect unless a supermajority of Congress changed or blocked them, any proposed cost reductions could not exceed 0.5 percent of Medicare spending in 2015, a threshold that increases gradually to 1.5 percent of spending in 2018 and beyond. Congress also wrote into law a provision that protects hospitals in the near term by prohibiting IPAB from reducing hospital rates before 2019.

Given the restrictions on its cost-reducing activities, it remains to be seen whether the IPAB will be effective. But history is not promising. Medicare already features a type of spending cap that has not worked very well. It's called the Sustainable Growth Rate (SGR) and is designed to automatically reduce Medicare's reimbursement rates to physicians when payments rise above a certain target. But every year for more than a decade, Congress has refused to implement scheduled reductions in Medicare payments to doctors. The cuts were initially modest, but because Congress has refused to act year after year, the potential cuts have become larger and more politically difficult to enact.

Market-based approaches to Medicare spending also have been proposed. Typically, such proposals would give seniors a fixed subsidy—or voucher—to buy insurance in the private market. The idea behind such proposals is that if consumers shop for insurance plans that offered the best value, market forces would reward efficient providers and squeeze out the inefficient ones, just as markets work in other sectors. To be sure, fixed subsidies would stabilize the federal government's healthcare expenditures (because the costs would be specified). However, unless there's a stabilization of the overall cost of healthcare, either (1) seniors would be forced to pay more out of pocket for healthcare or (2) the fixed subsidies would go up, and the budgetary savings implied by the reform wouldn't materialize. Still, this approach is interesting enough that we should consider experimenting with them to better understand how they might affect healthcare costs and quality. In fact, the new health insurance exchanges will give us some information about the advantages and limitations of providing subsidies to individuals for insurance.

Reducing system-wide health spending will also be vital to controlling the cost of Medicaid, which is a joint federal-state program that pays for health insurance for those with low incomes. According to the Kaiser Family Foundation, nearly three quarters of Medicaid beneficiaries (including children and their parents) are enrolled in some form of managed care, which, unlike fee-for-service, controls costs by establishing a network of designated or preferred providers, reviewing the utilization of health services to limit unnecessary care, and providing incentives for efficient use of medical services. But according to some estimates, enrollees in managed-care plans represent less than 30 percent of Medicaid's costs. Of the more expensive beneficiaries—the elderly and disabled who need intermediate and long-term care—only 10 percent have managed-care arrangements. This situation has started to change: over half of the states now contract with managed-care organizations with capitated payments for long-term care.

To contain Medicaid costs at the federal level (which account for about 60 percent of Medicaid's total spending), some have proposed providing block grants to the states, which administer the program and share in its financing. Under such a scenario, it would be up to state lawmakers to adapt their state's program to operate with a fixed federal contribution that would grow at a predetermined annual rate (supplemented by each state's own contribution). Again, the overall sustainability of such a proposal could be limited until we figure out how to restrain cost growth throughout the entire healthcare system and address the potential effects on the access to healthcare services by Medicaid beneficiaries. Nonetheless, the proposal is promising because many states are adept at finding innovative solutions to difficult problems.

# DEVELOPING COST CURES AT THE PETERSON CENTER ON HEALTHCARE

The Peterson Center on Healthcare (PCH) will be a major new initiative of our foundation, focused on raising the performance of the U.S. healthcare industry by improving outcomes while also lowering costs. While many organizations are focused on improving other aspects of healthcare (such as access or quality), relatively few have our significant emphasis on costs. Improving the performance and efficiency of our delivery system is an essential part of a long-term solution to our nation's rising healthcare costs. As the Peterson Institute for International Economics did when it became established thirty years ago and focused on increasing our understanding of and informing people about the international economy, PCH will focus on improving our understanding of how healthcare, a critical component of our economy, affects our nation's overall economic well-being. Over time, my hope is that this organization will become a trusted and reliable catalyst toward improving healthcare and lowering costs in this vital sector of the U.S. economy.

We have recruited a top advisory board, which is chaired by Dr. Harvey Fineberg, the former president of the Institute of Medicine, and includes highly influential leaders from various healthcare organizations in America. Among these experts are the heads of the Cleveland Clinic and the Geisinger health system, both of whom have demonstrated the feasibility of achieving better outcomes at lower cost.

A key component of our work will be to accelerate the velocity of improvement in healthcare by identifying and validating high-impact solutions that reduce costs and improve outcomes. We will then facilitate the adoption of these high-value practices on a national scale. We plan to collaborate with healthcare providers and other key stakeholders around the country to adopt and scale up more efficient practices and innovations.

In addition, PCH will work to foster the conditions for the healthcare sector to change and improve. PCH will support activities to build a better overall environment for healthcare performance improvement, including increasing awareness and urgency of the need for change, enhancing data transparency, driving innovation toward higher-value healthcare, and developing incentives that reward efficiency. To help facilitate conditions for better performance, PCH will work on systemic initiatives to drive greater motivation among stakeholders to improve and innovate, including work in the areas of: data transparency and information, value versus volume–based reimbursement, and value-based benefits design that drives greater consumer involvement and price sensitivity.

PCH will work with significant stakeholders in both the private and public sector, including providers, payers, and consumer advocacy groups. We will sponsor projects in key areas of the delivery system, such as population-based primary care, integrated care for high-cost patients, and advanced illness care.

Our work has already begun. One organization that we support is Stanford's Clinical Excellence Research Center (CERC). Led by Dr. Arnold Milstein, CERC has been traveling around the country to find healthcare providers whose innovations produce high-quality healthcare at lower costs. The initial results are promising. For example, the Stanford team found a primary care group that monitors patients closely when they are cared for by other providers and is able to improve healthcare and lower costs through better coordination of services. Other physician groups identified by CERC use their highly trained specialists when they are needed the most while routine care is provided by other group members. Stanford found another provider group that uses an innovative clinic to deliver primary care to Medicaid patients who might otherwise go to expensive emergency rooms. As these and other innovations are identified and fully validated, our center will work to drive their adoption and replication in healthcare organizations across the nation.

Another planned PCH initiative will help draw attention to the latest data on industrywide performance in the healthcare sector. In collaboration with the Kaiser Family Foundation led by Dr. Drew Altman, this project will highlight spending trends as well as emerging public and private efforts to control costs and improve quality. The project will introduce an easy-to-use website to facilitate the access to this information by key stakeholders and the public, and will include a range of interactive tools that help users better understand the data and emerging trends in healthcare.

To sum up, I believe that reducing healthcare spending while achieving equal or better health outcomes is an essential part of building a better economy and solving our nation's long-term fiscal challenges. By developing its leadership, expertise, and unique focus in this area, the Peterson Center on Healthcare will aim to become a leading catalyst in facilitating the transformation of U.S. healthcare into a high-performing industry. We have an enormous opportunity in front of us to improve the health of millions of Americans while reducing costs at the same time. This is a challenge we simply must address.

# 5

# FIGHTING FOR OUR FUTURE

## Getting More from Every Defense Dollar

One of the major lessons from history is that a nation's security ultimately depends on its economic strength. To have a strong economy and a strong nation, we must put our federal budget back on a sustainable path and tackle the mounting challenge of our long-term debt.

I do not believe there has ever been a closer link among fiscal security, economic security, and national security. And I'm not alone. As Admiral Mike Mullen, the former chairman of the Joint Chiefs of Staff, has said, "The single, biggest threat to our national security is our debt."

Moreover, as the following chart indicates, the United States currently spends more than $600 billion annually on defense—more than the next eight countries combined, according to data collected by the Stockholm International Peace Research

# THE UNITED STATES SPENDS MORE ON DEFENSE THAN THE NEXT EIGHT COUNTRIES COMBINED

**Defense Spending** (Billions of dollars)

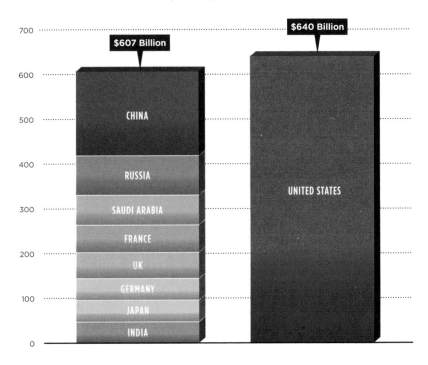

SOURCE: Stockholm International Peace Research Institute, *SIPRI Military Expenditure Database,* April 2014. Data are for 2013. Compiled by PGPF.
NOTE: Figures are in U.S. dollars, converted from local currencies using market exchange rates.

Institute. Given these staggering numbers, it is hard to imagine that the United States is getting its money's worth.

The winding down of our engagements in Iraq and Afghanistan presented a unique opportunity to rethink our defense strategy and spending priorities. But we largely squandered that opportunity. Although defense spending has been put on a declining path for the next decade as a share of GDP, the reductions in spending to date have not been made strategically. For example, the Department of Defense (DoD) was forced to implement a set of across-the-board cuts in 2013 as a result of that year's sequester. The defense sequester required an equal reduction across many defense programs, whether the program was crucial to today's national security or not (with a notable exception of military pay, which was exempt from sequestration). That's a poor way to reduce defense spending, let alone defend the country.

We can do better. Instead of continuing to make arbitrary across-the-board cuts to the defense budget, the United States needs to set a new defense strategy that can help guide our nation's spending decisions about the best way to protect our national security against the threats of the twenty-first century.

Fortunately, many experts in both parties believe now is the time for a top-to-bottom review of defense strategy, particularly in light of the changing global security landscape, advances in military technology over the past few decades, and the reality that future budget constraints will demand smarter prioritization of defense spending. In December 2012, the Coalition for Fiscal and National Security, a distinguished bipartisan group of former high-level government officials brought together by the Peterson Foundation, issued a statement highlighting how strategic needs have evolved in this new era:

"In previous eras, increased defense spending may have been required to maintain security. That is no longer the case. In our judgment, advances in technological capabilities and

# Addressing Our Debt is a National Security Imperative

## A message from the new Coalition for Fiscal and National Security

We are former senior government officials who have served during eight Presidential administrations, Democratic and Republican, and former leaders in Congress from both parties. We join together now because we strongly believe that our long-term debt is the single greatest threat to our national security, and we urge elected leaders to agree by the end of this year on a plan that both averts the fiscal cliff and puts the debt on a downward path.

U.S. national security in the 21st century rests on both economic and military strength, for our military might and diplomatic muscle ultimately depend on a vibrant economy. Unless we change course, our huge and growing debt will undermine our economic growth, our military strength, and our global leadership.

Our leaders should use the consensus against going over the fiscal cliff as an opportunity to agree now on a framework for significant fiscal reform in 2013. Another "kicking of the can" — the lowest common denominator of what both parties can currently accept, without any structural reforms that truly address the nation's problems — is not acceptable. We must reassure our own citizens and businesses, the international financial markets, and the greater global community that America will address its fundamental challenges and maintain its leadership role in the world.

At a minimum, the resolution of the fiscal cliff by the end of the year should have the following components:

- The Objective: Our fiscal goal must be to stabilize the debt as a share of the economy, and put it on a downward path for the longer term. We cannot continue to grow our national debt faster than our economy if we want to maintain our global leadership. Any solution which does not meet this simple test is insufficient.

- The Framework: To achieve this objective, our leaders should decide on a fiscal framework that results in substantial deficit reduction over the next 10 years and structural changes to our fiscal policies that eventually balance the budget over the long term, including:

  - Specific levels of revenue, spending and deficits over the next 10 years, and parameters for longer-term fiscal reform, including future levels of debt as a share of the economy, and a date by which the budget must balance.

  - Tax reforms to raise more revenues, encourage growth and enhance progressivity — and it must be decided how much should be done through eliminating deductions, increasing rates and/or more fundamental changes to our tax code.

  - Changes to entitlements to put them on a sustainable long-term path, as well as changes to defense and other discretionary spending, while protecting the most vulnerable and preserving sufficient resources to invest in the future.

    - In our judgment, advances in technological capabilities and the changing nature of threats make it possible, if properly done, to spend less on a more intelligent, efficient and contemporary defense strategy that maintains our military superiority and national security.

- The Process: Congress and the President should agree on an expedited process to enact legislation reflecting this framework in 2013, including appropriate default and enforcement mechanisms that ensure we will achieve the targeted result.

In a time of division and drift, the true test for America is neither military nor economic — it is political. We ask our elected officials from both parties to assert genuine leadership, communicate to the American people what needs to be done, and make pragmatic policy decisions to power our nation's economy, democracy, and role in the world. It will require courage, shared sacrifice and a willingness to compromise and make the tough choices essential to setting a new course for our nation. It summons the truest form of patriotism — putting our country first.

## The Coalition for Fiscal and National Security

**Admiral Michael G. Mullen** (U.S. Navy, Ret.)
Coalition Chairman
former Chairman of the Joint Chiefs of Staff

**Madeleine K. Albright**
former Secretary of State

**James A. Baker, III**
former Secretary of State
and the Treasury

**Samuel R. Berger**
former National Security Advisor

**Harold Brown**
former Secretary of Defense

**Zbigniew Brzezinski**
former National Security Advisor

**Frank Carlucci**
former Secretary of Defense

**Robert M. Gates**
former Secretary of Defense

**Henry A. Kissinger**
former Secretary of State
and National Security Advisor

**Sam Nunn**
former Chairman of the Senate
Committee on Armed Services

**Paul O'Neill**
former Secretary of the Treasury

**George P. Shultz**
former Secretary of State
and the Treasury

**Ike Skelton**
former Chairman of the House
Committee on Armed Services

**Paul Volcker**
former Chairman of
the Federal Reserve

**John Warner**
former Chairman of the Senate
Committee on Armed Services

To read a more detailed message from the Coalition, please visit
**www.FiscalAndNationalSecurity.org**

Peter G. Peterson
Foundation
Our America. Our Future.

the changing nature of threats make it possible, if properly done, to spend less on a more intelligent, efficient and contemporary defense strategy that maintains our military superiority and national security."*

The statement emphasizes that if the United States fails to strategize now for how to best meet our national security needs in a new fiscal and economic era, we will eventually undermine our economy, military strength, and global leadership. Our defense strategy should not be an accounting exercise.

# A NEW, SMARTER STRATEGY

To help answer the need for a twenty-first-century defense strategy, the Peterson Foundation provided financial support to and partnered with the Stimson Center to convene the Defense Advisory Committee, a group of top-level military and diplomatic experts. The committee issued recommendations designed to modernize U.S. military strategy and prepare for new and emerging threats. Their recommendations are included in a report entitled "A New U.S. Defense Strategy for a New Era: Military Superiority, Agility, and Efficiency," which spells out how to maintain America's dominant defensive ca-

---

*Coalition for Fiscal and National Security, "Addressing Our Debt: A National Security Imperative" (December 2012), www.FiscalandNational Security.org.

pabilities at a lower financial cost.* The committee issued a second report in September 2013 detailing specific ways that the Defense Department could implement this strategy to meet the budget caps and sequester facing the Defense Department.†

At the heart of this recommended strategy is a more flexible U.S. presence around the world. This new strategy is rooted in the unprecedented agility, technological superiority, and global reach of modern U.S. armed forces—especially through naval, air, and space power. It also recognizes fundamental and emerging national security needs such as protecting our critical civilian, government, and military infrastructure from cyber attack; securing vital sea lanes; and countering the nuclear threat from belligerent nations and terrorists while safely reducing the size and cost of our own force structure and nuclear arsenal.

Under such a strategy, ground forces would be deployed into combat far less frequently, and only with well-defined and limited objectives. The Defense Advisory Committee argues that a more focused use of fighting forces would make it possible to reduce the number of personnel in our ground forces by as much as one third.

---

* Stimson Center, "A New U.S. Defense Strategy for a New Era: Military Superiority, Agility, and Efficiency" (Washington, D.C.: Stimson Center, November 2012). www.stimson.org/books-reports/a-new-us-defense-strategy-for-a-new-era-military-superiority-agility-and-efficiency/.

† Stimson Center, "Strong National Defense for Today's Global and Fiscal Realities" (Washington, D.C.: Stimson Center, September 2013). www.stimson.org/books-reports/strategic-agility-strong-national-defense-for-todays-global-and-fiscal-realities/.

This approach would implement the hard and costly lessons about the limits of military power that our nation learned after more than a decade of war. As Robert Gates, who served as defense secretary for presidents George W. Bush and Barack Obama, said, "Any future defense secretary who advises the president to again send a big American land army into Asia or into the Middle East or Africa should 'have his head examined,' as General MacArthur so delicately put it."

The new strategy would place increased emphasis on the National Guard and the reserves. Although the committee recommends avoiding protracted ground wars, we live in a world full of uncertainties and the reserve forces would serve as a hedge against the possibility of a major ground operation in the future. The National Guard and the reserves can provide an insurance policy for just such contingencies, offering a cost-effective way to complement the active force temporarily in times of great need. The ground forces in the Guard and the selected reserves number six hundred thousand—enough to supplement active-duty forces if the need arises, and to ensure that hard-learned capabilities like counterinsurgency war fighting don't erode. This shift can save money because DoD's total wage and benefit costs for each active-duty service member are about $108,000 per year, versus about $34,000 per year for each reservist (when not on active duty).

With a smaller ground force, our troops could be regularly rotated through smaller bases in other countries without requiring as many expensive permanent bases as we have today. Such a strategy would allow us to maintain an ongoing presence in critical regions such as Asia, where our presence must remain robust, given the risks posed by North Korea's nuclear program and China's growing assertiveness in global affairs. By maintaining a lighter footprint in other politically sensitive regions, the United States would also be less likely to exacerbate resentment among populations that may be hostile to our presence. Additionally, with fewer fixed bases around the world and shorter rotations of defense personnel abroad, family members could remain at home, which would reduce costs.

Any new strategy should also be focused on addressing the true threats of today and those emerging in the years ahead. We will need to increase spending in areas that can counter those threats, which now range from sophisticated terror attacks to cyber attacks to any number of other diffuse national security threats. This strategy will require a more modern, agile military that has the resources it needs for special operations forces, cyber warfare, and the basic and applied research and development that will keep our forces the most informed, best equipped, and best trained in the world.

The experience of the last decade taught a painful lesson: the U.S. military should fight wars only when necessary, and not be tempted into protracted land wars or nation-building exercises. Whatever one thinks of the U.S. military campaigns in Iraq and Afghanistan, it's clear that they've been an enormous strain on the U.S. budget. The Peterson Foundation estimates that the total cost of these two efforts—including related future spending—will be about two trillion dollars (though some researchers have estimated the cost is even higher). Over the same period, that is equivalent to about 70 percent of total federal spending on research and development, which should be a high priority for the United States in an increasingly technological world economy.

It will also be important for our friends and allies to increase their contributions—both military and financial—to our common defense. It is past time for our allies to understand that we are willing to play a leadership role in global security, but that we will not use our budget to subsidize their responsibilities. In 2013, the United States spent about 3.8 percent of GDP on defense, versus 1 to 2 percent by most of our European allies (down from 2 to 3 percent in the 1990s), according to data collected by the Stockholm International Peace Research Institute.

## THE UNITED STATES HISTORICALLY DEVOTES A LARGER SHARE OF ITS ECONOMY TO DEFENSE THAN MANY OF ITS KEY ALLIES

**Defense Spending** (Percentage of GDP)

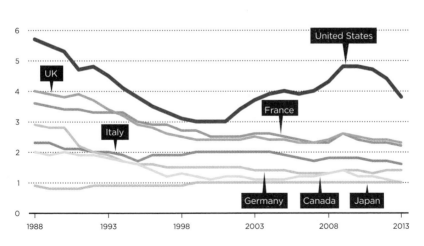

**SOURCE:** Stockholm International Peace Research Institute, *SIPRI Military Expenditure Database,* April 2014. Compiled by PGPF.

Despite an agreement that the NATO allies will spend 2 percent of their GDP on defense, only three countries among NATO's twenty-eight members met that criterion in 2013.

With the right strategy in place, we can devote less of our economic output to defense and still safeguard our global security interests. At the same time, our allies—particularly our partners in NATO and East Asia—should enhance their defense capabilities to ensure they contribute their fair share to maintaining security in critical regions.

United States defense spending is now on a declining path as a share of GDP. I am glad to see that defense spending is no longer considered a sacred cow. For too long, Pentagon planners have been allergic to setting budget priorities—and no one in Congress or the White House has forced them to do so. Our nation's security must be a top priority for the federal government. But no agency, including the Pentagon, should have a blank check. To quote Admiral Mullen again, "[The Pentagon] budget has basically doubled in the last decade. And . . . in that doubling, we've lost our ability to prioritize, to make hard decisions, to do tough analysis, to make trades." I was pleased to see that the proposal from the Pentagon in early 2014 includes many of the recommendations of the Defense Advisory Committee.

## FINDING EFFICIENCIES TO DO MORE WITH LESS

"Waste, fraud, and abuse" is a favorite mantra of those who think that closing budget gaps should be an easy exercise. Most of the time, it turns out that the savings from such cuts amount to just a sliver of the overall challenge. But in the case of military spending, there truly is a tremendous amount of money at stake in simply making the department run better and more efficiently. The Defense Advisory Committee found nearly $1 trillion in potential savings over ten years in the defense budget.

One of the first goals should be to reduce overhead expenses and find new efficiencies in the way we manage the Defense Department. The military members of the Stimson Center panel felt particularly strongly that the military has too much overhead—such as overspending on headquarters rather than on training, equipment, and war fighting.

Examples of efficiency savings include measures such as reducing the number of defense contractors, eliminating unnecessary overhead and duplicative support staff, transferring more commercial jobs from armed forces personnel to others, and closing or selling underused or unused facilities. Another area to examine closely is the civilian defense workforce. Civilians make critical contributions to our national defense. Yet between 2001 and 2012, civilian employment at the DoD grew 17 percent, while active-duty military personnel levels grew by only 3.4 percent.* The Defense Advisory Committee believes that these numbers can safely be reduced.

All of these changes should be combined with aggressive efforts to reform military procurement and eliminate un-

---

*Gordon Adams and others, "Consensus on Defense Reforms," American Enterprise Institute, June 3, 2013, http://www.aei.org/article/foreign-and-defense-policy/defense/consensus-on-defense-reforms/.

needed equipment. For instance, the Defense Advisory Committee nearly unanimously agreed that future purchases of the costly F-35 fighter jet could be reduced without compromising U.S. air power. Each plane costs $135 million.

The committee also agreed that a significant share of the nation's intercontinental ballistic missiles (ICBMs) should be retired, while still maintaining enough warheads to provide an adequate nuclear deterrent. Given today's security environment, we do not need to maintain a massive nuclear arsenal.

Scholars from across the political spectrum have also focused on the need to reform the system of military pay and benefits. Many have stressed the need to reform these systems before they devour our military capabilities. From 2001 to 2012, the compensation cost per active-duty service member grew 56 percent after adjusting for inflation.* In testimony before the House Appropriations Committee, former defense secretary Robert Gates said that "the Defense Department runs the risk of the fate of other corporate and government bureaucracies that were ultimately crippled by personnel costs, in particular, their retiree benefit packages." Another issue: retirement benefits are provided for those with twenty or more years of service, but are not available for those with fewer than twenty years of service. According to the Defense Business Board, only 17 percent of military personnel serve the twenty years necessary to draw retirement while those who leave earlier—including many of those who served in Iraq and

---

* Gordon Adams and others, "Consensus on Defense Reforms."

Afghanistan—get no military retirement benefits. The system could be reformed by reallocating the benefits between these two groups and slowing the growth of overall retirement costs. Given the political sensitivities involved in reducing defense personnel costs, Congress chartered a commission to review retirement and military pay and benefits. My hope is that Congress will take the commission's recommendations seriously.

The sacrifices made by men and women in the military and their families go far above and beyond what most Americans can even imagine, and we have a corresponding obligation to provide for the needs of those who have sacrificed most. We must ensure that our wounded warriors have the best healthcare available. But most of the spending on our military health programs does not go to wounded warriors. Moreover, the gap between the health benefits provided by the private sector and the military has grown considerably. If changes are not made, the costs of those benefits will impose an even larger burden on future defense budgets. One problem: military retirees and their dependents pay only a fraction of what civilians pay for healthcare, which creates incentives for unnecessary and expensive care. We need to slow the growth of military health costs, maintain a high quality of care provided to our service members, and ensure that this important health system remains financially viable for the long run.

Just as a rifle without bullets is not so useful, neither is a military without a strong economy to sustain it over the long term. Defense dollars are essential, and they obviously have to come from somewhere. That's why we must insist that our leaders be realistic and honest about the threats that America now faces—including that of long-term debt and its effect on national security in the decades ahead.

The changes outlined in this chapter would result in a more modern and efficient Department of Defense, one well prepared to tackle today's security threats, confront our fiscal realities, and ensure that America's economic strength is preserved.

| ORIGINAL MEMBERS OF THE DEFENSE ADVISORY COMMITTEE | |
|---|---|
| Barry M. Blechman | Cofounder and Distinguished Fellow, Stimson Center |
| Professor Gordon Adams | Professor of International Relations, School of International Service, American University; Distinguished Fellow, Stimson Center |
| Professor Graham Allison | Douglas Dillon Professor of Government, John F. Kennedy School of Government, Harvard University; Director, Belfer Center for Science and International Affairs, Harvard University |
| Michael J. Bayer | President and CEO, Dumbarton Strategies |
| General B. B. Bell, USA (Ret.) | Former Commander UNC/CFC/USFK, Republic of Korea |
| Professor Richard K. Betts | Director, Arnold A. Saltzman Institute of War and Peace Studies, Columbia University |
| Ambassador Lincoln P. Bloomfield Jr. | Chairman, Stimson Center |

| | |
|---|---|
| Ambassador Richard Burt | Managing Director, McLarty Associates<br><br>Cochairman, Global Zero |
| General James Cartwright, USMC (Ret.) | Harold Brown Chair in Defense Policy Studies, Center for Strategic and International Studies |
| Lieutenant General Daniel W. Christman, USA (Ret.) | Senior Counselor, US Chamber of Commerce |
| Lieutenant General David A. Deptula, USAF (Ret.) | Senior Military Scholar, Center for Character and Leadership Development, United States Air Force Academy |
| Leslie H. Gelb | President Emeritus and Board Senior Fellow, Council on Foreign Relations |
| Jessica T. Mathews | President, Carnegie Endowment for International Peace |
| Admiral Bill Owens, USN (Ret.) | Prometheus Partners |
| Professor Anne-Marie Slaughter | Bert G. Kerstetter '66 University Professor Emerita of Politics and International Affairs, Princeton University |
| **Additional Members in the Expanded Defense Advisory Committee** | |
| Philip A. Odeen | Former Chairman and CEO, TRW Inc. |
| Admiral Gary Roughead, USN (Ret.) | Former Chief of Naval Operations |
| General Norton Schwartz, USAF (Ret.) | Former Air Force Chief of Staff |

# 6

## GETTING BACK ON COURSE

### Options for Raising Revenue

A s the eminent Supreme Court justice Oliver Wendell Holmes Jr. once noted, "Taxes are what we pay for a civilized society." And while we don't like to pay them, virtually all of us enjoy the benefits they yield, even if we never make the explicit connection between our tax bills and those benefits. Whether it's for groundbreaking medical studies, GPS satellite navigation, weather forecasting, twenty-four-hour air traffic control, reliable transportation infrastructure, port security, or a strong military, tax revenue pays for many essential day-to-day operations of our nation and its economy. And tax revenue funds important entitlement benefits, such as Social Security, Medicare, and Medicaid.

We tend to take for granted all of the benefits we receive until something goes wrong, a government service is substandard, or some program or tax break that we like is suddenly cut. Unfortunately, these unpleasant possibilities are likely to become more and more common in coming decades, as there is a growing mismatch between the tax revenue that will come in under current policy and the cost of providing the services that millions of Americans have come to expect. As noted earlier, this mismatch—if left unaddressed—will produce more and more debt and related interest costs, so much so that it will threaten our nation's prosperity, our safety net, and our global leadership.

I know some people believe we should simply cut spending to match the level of revenue. But as I showed in chapter 2, this approach could carry severe consequences for government programs that are important for economic growth and vulnerable populations. Moreover, for any reform plan to be viable over the long term, it must be bipartisan. Practically speaking, any "grand bargain" to reduce long-term debt will have to include revenues in order to gain sufficient support among Democrats, along with spending cuts to bring Republicans on board. Several bipartisan groups have proposed raising revenues. For example, the report by the bipartisan National Commission on Fiscal Responsibility and Reform, cochaired by Alan Simpson and Erskine Bowles, proposed increasing federal revenues to 21 percent of GDP in the long run—substantially higher than their fifty-year historical average of 17.3 percent.

The best way for the government to collect more revenues is through increased receipts that result from a faster growing economy. For that reason, it is important for fiscal policy to promote, rather than discourage, growth. In fact, our current tax system has evolved into a complicated set of laws and regulations that reward some behaviors and penalize others, which can distort economic decision making. Ideally, any long-term fiscal plan that includes additional revenue would include comprehensive tax reform that not only makes the tax code simpler and fairer, but also is progrowth.

It is important to point out that there is a difference between raising revenues and raising marginal tax *rates*. These are not one and the same. For example, some tax reforms could help the economy grow faster, which in turn could raise revenues. Indeed, one way to help garner Republican support for revenue increases is through more comprehensive tax reform that reduces tax expenditures and lowers tax rates.

Some people argue that raising taxes by any amount would discourage investors and entrepreneurs, and thus choke off the capital and spirit that fuel America's economic engine. I don't believe that to be true. Even many people on Wall Street agree.

Given the growing disparity of income in America, I believe that generating more tax revenue (as part of a grand bargain) should of course include raising revenue from those of us in the upper income brackets. I believe the well off—myself included—should not only have to pay more in taxes but should also receive less in benefits. We benefited far more than all other Americans over the past several decades, and now we should be willing to take the lead in fixing America's unsustainable budget. Even though our long-term problems cannot be solved by raising top tax rates alone (as I showed in chapter 2), it will be essential, as a matter of fairness as well as political viability, that people with higher incomes make greater sacrifices as part of a successful fiscal plan.

Warren Buffet has proposed a minimum tax rate of 30 percent on the incomes of people earning more than a million dollars per year. Although this tax would generate only about $100 billion of additional revenue over ten years—which is small in comparison to our ten-year $7.2 trillion deficits under current law—it would convey an important message that well-off Americans were doing their full part to help the United States solve its long-term budgetary challenges.

Another example of an action that could rebalance perceptions about the tax code would be eliminating the so-called carried interest provision, which allows private equity managers to treat labor income as low-taxed capital gains. This provision is nearly impossible to justify as these gains are almost entirely for services rendered and not for return on capital.

Recent history suggests that revenues can be raised in a sensible and balanced way that does not stifle growth. As I discussed earlier, in the 1990s during the administrations of George H. W. Bush and Bill Clinton, America raised taxes on higher earners in combination with spending caps, PAYGO rules (which required that legislated increases in mandatory spending or cuts to revenues be offset so as to not raise the deficit), and other tools to enforce budget discipline. These policy changes certainly did not devastate economic growth. After their enactment, the U.S. economy boomed throughout the 1990s, and the federal government ran four consecutive budget surpluses from 1998 to 2001. In part, this budget discipline on both the spending and revenue side boosted confidence in the capital markets, which contributed to economic growth.

Former Federal Reserve chairman Paul Volcker agrees. At a forum the Peterson Foundation hosted after the 2012 election, I asked Volcker how much damage a reasonable upper-income tax increase would inflict on the economy. His answer? "Zero."

Many of us fear that, as part of a budget agreement to tackle long-term debt, taxes will go up but that corresponding spending cuts will never be implemented. To help build the trust necessary for compromise, revenue increases and spending reforms should be packaged together in legislation. We also need protections to ensure that a spending cut one year is not simply offset with a spending increase the following year. The 1983 bipartisan Social Security reform package provides a good model. It included both revenue increases and long-term changes that reduced Social Security benefits and raised the retirement age over time. The reform has stood the test of time because both elements—tax increases and spending cuts—were included in the legislation together, and both parties agreed to abide by their compromise.

Policymakers might also consider the recommendations of the Peterson-Pew Commission on Budget Reform, which developed a three-part framework to ensure that both promised spending cuts and tax increases are actually implemented. The commission recommended that: (1) Congress set medium-term targets for the federal debt as a percentage of GDP; (2) that the president be required to submit a budget to meet those targets; and (3) that across-the-board spending cuts *and* tax increases be automatically triggered if future lawmakers fail to adhere to the targets. (These automatic changes differ significantly from the sequester because they would include taxes and not exempt any spending program.) The framework would allow the automatic spending cuts and tax hikes to be waived only in times of war or recession. I believe triggers along these lines could give both sides assurance that a deal made today will endure over the long haul.


# REFORMING THE INCOME TAX CODE

As lawmakers look for ways to find additional revenue, a top priority should be revising and streamlining the current income tax code, which is riddled with loopholes, deductions, subsidies, credits, and other market-distorting special provisions that make the system unnecessarily complex and virtually incomprehensible to ordinary taxpayers. Many economists agree that broadening the tax base by trimming the tax code's many deductions and exclusions would improve, not impair, economic efficiency.

I strongly support the bipartisan Simpson-Bowles Commission's recommendation to scale back or eliminate most "tax expenditures"—many of which are nothing more than "spending in disguise."* The following chart shows just how large these tax expenditures have become in comparison with the rest of the budget.

---

*Donald B. Marron, "Spending in Disguise," *National Affairs* 8 (Summer 2011): 20–34.

## CORPORATE AND INDIVIDUAL TAX EXPENDITURES ARE LARGE IN COMPARISON WITH ANNUAL TAXES COLLECTED AS WELL AS WITH THE GOVERNMENT'S MAJOR PROGRAMS

**Budgetary Impact** (Billions of dollars)

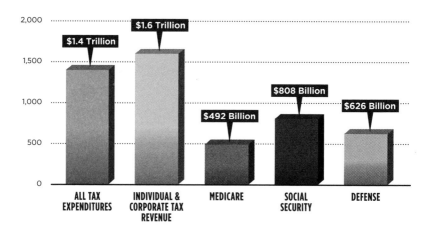

SOURCE: Office of Management and Budget, *Budget of the United States Government, Fiscal Year 2015,* March 2014. Data are for 2013. Compiled by PGPF.
NOTE: Medicare spending is net of premiums and payments from the states. Those receipts were $93 billion in 2013. Income tax revenue includes both individual and corporate income tax receipts. Tax expenditures include deductions, credits, exclusions, and preferential rates, and the data reflect the effects on outlays, payroll, and excise taxes.

This vast panoply of tax breaks and disguised backdoor spending amounts to $1.4 trillion a year—more than the federal government spends each year on Social Security, Medicare, or Defense, or approaching the total amount of revenue collected from individual and corporate income taxes combined. They also flow disproportionately to the more affluent. According to the CBO, the top 1 percent of taxpayers receives 17 percent of the value of the major tax expenditures in the individual income tax code. However, the top 1 percent also is responsible for 46 percent of the individual income tax revenue collected by the federal government.

To address these distortions and reduce their fiscal impact, we need to trim not just low-hanging fruit, such as corporate and individual tax loopholes, but also take a hard look at popular and large individual tax breaks, such as the interest deduction for mortgages (up to $1 million), and the exclusion of

## THE TOP 1 PERCENT OF TAXPAYERS CLAIM 17 PERCENT OF THE TOTAL VALUE OF MAJOR TAX EXPENDITURES

**Distribution of Major Individual Income Tax Expenditures**

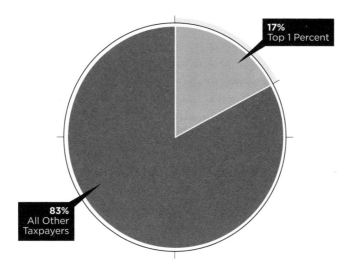

17%
Top 1 Percent

83%
All Other
Taxpayers

SOURCE: Congressional Budget Office, *The Distribution of Major Tax Expenditures in the Individual Income Tax System,* May 2013. Compiled by PGPF.

# THE TOP 1 PERCENT OF TAXPAYERS GENERATE 46 PERCENT OF INDIVIDUAL INCOME TAX REVENUE

### Share of Individual Income Tax

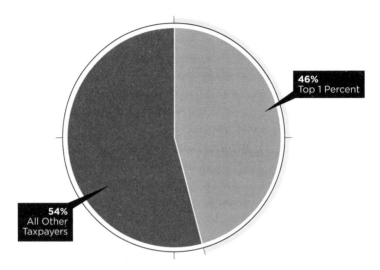

**46%** Top 1 Percent

**54%** All Other Taxpayers

**SOURCE:** Tax Policy Center, *Table T13-0180—Share of Federal Taxes by Filing Status by Expanded Cash Income Percentile,* July 2013. Data are for 2014. Compiled by PGPF.

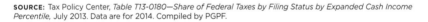

employer-paid health insurance from federal taxation (a provision that also drives up healthcare costs). These popular tax breaks account for most of the total cost of all tax expenditures. In fact, corporate tax expenditures account for less than 15 percent of the total cost of all tax expenditures. By contrast, just five popular tax breaks for individuals account for about half of the total costs—or about $665 billion annually, as the following chart shows.

## FIVE INDIVIDUAL TAX PROVISIONS ACCOUNT FOR MORE THAN $665 BILLION IN ANNUAL INCOME TAX EXPENDITURES

| 5 MAJOR TAX EXPENDITURES | BUDGETARY COSTS (FY 2013) |
|---|---|
| 1. Exclusion of employer contributions for medical insurance and care* | $303 Billion |
| 2. Exclusion of pension contributions and earnings† | $128 Billion |
| 3. Lower rates on dividends and long-term capital gains | $93 Billion |
| 4. Deduction for state and local taxes | $73 Billion |
| 5. Deduction of mortgage interest on owner-occupied homes with loan values up to $1 million | $69 Billion |
| TOTAL | $667 Billion |

SOURCE: Office of Management and Budget, *Budget of the United States Government, Fiscal Year 2015,* March 2014. Data are for 2013. Compiled by PGPF.
NOTE: Numbers do not sum to totals because of rounding. *Includes the exclusion from payroll taxes and income taxes. †Includes employer pension plans, employee and employer contributions to 401(k) plans, IRAs, and self-employed plans.

# REFORMING THE CORPORATE INCOME TAX CODE

Just as we need to reform the personal income tax, we need to reform the corporate income tax too. The tax rate on U.S. corporations is the highest in the developed world.

As a consequence, it distorts the behavior of many companies in inefficient ways, as those companies seek to exploit the differential between U.S. and foreign tax rates through offshore accounting maneuvers. Corporations divert resources

# THE STATUTORY TAX RATE ON U.S. CORPORATIONS IS THE HIGHEST IN THE DEVELOPED WORLD

### Combined Corporate Income Tax Rate

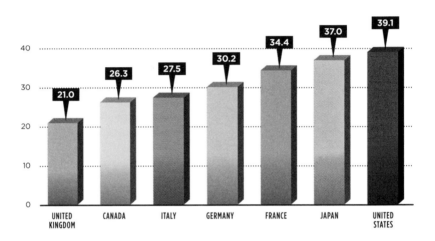

**SOURCE:** Organization for Economic Cooperation and Development, *Tax Database,* May 2014. Compiled by PGPF.
**NOTE:** Data are from 2014 and reflect the basic combined national and subnational statutory corporate income tax rate. Japan cut the central government portion of its corporate income tax rate on April 1, 2012, to 28.05 percent, which includes a temporary 10 percent surtax that was set to expire after three years. During FY2014 tax reform, the Japanese government decided that the surtax will expire one year ahead of schedule. The nations depicted here represent the G-7.

from making and selling goods and services to hiring tax attorneys, accountants, and lobbyists to minimize tax obligations. The high corporate tax rate has also encouraged a large number of companies to organize as LLCs (limited liability corporations), S corporations, and partnerships so they can avoid paying the corporate tax and instead pass their income directly to their owners, where it is taxed at the individual level. More than half of all U.S. firms are not organized as businesses subject to the corporate tax.

Because of these tax avoidance behaviors and the availability of various deductions and credits that enable corporations to further reduce their tax liabilities, the U.S. corporate income tax system is relatively inefficient in raising revenue. Indeed, despite our high statutory tax rates, the U.S. system does not raise as much revenue as the corporate tax systems in many other countries.

Also, because corporations can currently deduct interest payments when calculating taxable income but are prohibited from deducting dividend payments, corporations have an incentive to finance projects using debt rather than equity (equity is effectively double taxed in our current system—first at the corporate level and then as dividends or capital gains at the shareholder level). These distortions in corporate finance created by our tax system matter: although taking on debt helps reduce tax payments, it also makes corporations more vulnerable to economic fluctuations and increases the likelihood of default and bankruptcy.

Many analysts on both sides believe that we need to reform the corporate tax system, reduce the economic distortions it creates, and minimize the incentives for multinational corporations to shift jobs and profits to low-tax countries. Some have called for reducing the corporate income tax rate and eliminating loopholes to broaden the overall tax base, which I believe would be a step in the right direction. Such an approach could help to reduce tax distortions and bring U.S. rates more in line with those of our major trading partners, enhancing the competitiveness of U.S. corporations.

# THE CHALLENGE OF TAX REFORM

Reducing or eliminating big tax expenditures will be politically difficult. After all, most of these provisions are promoted by powerful entrenched interests with deep pockets for lobbyists, public relations firms, political action committees, and TV advertising. For instance, the mortgage interest deduction for mortgages up to $1 million is sacred to three of Washington's most influential advocacy groups—the National Association of Realtors, the Mortgage Bankers Association, and the National Association of Home Builders—not to mention millions of American households. With approximately 65 percent of American homes owner occupied, there's a huge constituency supporting a very costly status quo. But even the most ardent tax cutter should be able to recognize the value of reducing distortions in the tax code and making it more conducive to economic growth.

For reform of the individual income tax, one possible way to overcome some of the political battles associated with tax reform is to give taxpayers significant choice over which tax expenditures they want to use, but to set a cap on the overall savings individuals can realize from them in any given year. Under this approach, a person's tax deductions could not exceed a certain limit—either a fixed dollar amount or a percentage of income—and because no specific deduction would be targeted, opposition from special interests might be somewhat less intense.

Martin Feldstein, Maya MacGuineas, and Daniel Feenberg have proposed limiting the value of itemized deductions to no more than 2 percent of an individual's adjusted gross income.* The group estimated that this measure would have raised an additional $278 billion in 2011—half of what we spent on Medicare alone. Their analysis calculates that, under this plan, individuals with an income of more than $500,000 would pay an additional $40,000 on average.

Another proposal for reforming the individual income tax code calls for keeping tax rates where they are but capping itemized deductions at, for example, $50,000. The Tax Policy Center calculates that this change would generate about $750 billion in additional revenue over ten years, with more than 96 percent of the additional revenue coming from the top income quintile, and nearly 80 percent coming from the top 1 percent of income earners.

Similarly, President Obama has recommended limiting the tax benefit of each deduction to no more than 28 percent for all tax filers, rather than allowing wealthier earners to take a larger deduction at their higher marginal tax rate.

Regardless of which approach is taken, tax expenditure reforms should be phased in over a period of years to give recipients sufficient time to adjust. Many households have made important life decisions, such as taking a mortgage to buy a house, based on the tax code as it currently exists. By adjusting policy gradually, policymakers could reduce the economic disruptions of reform.

---

*Martin Feldstein, Daniel Feenberg, and Maya MacGuineas. "Capping Individual Tax Expenditure Benefits." NBER Working Paper 16921, Cambridge, MA, 2011.

## TAKING A FRESH LOOK

I am also rather intrigued by the so-called blank-slate proposal for tax expenditures, which has been supported by former senator Max Baucus and Senator Orrin Hatch, among others. Under this kind of approach, *all* tax expenditures would be eliminated. Members of Congress would then need to make the case for restoring specific tax breaks on an individual basis. Through this process, all tax expenditures would receive a review—something they rarely get.

A clean start like this is tempting, but it would require extraordinary transparency to ensure its integrity. This is because it inevitably favors those special interests with the most money to hire top lobbyists to persuade key elected officials, while constituencies without such resources or connections might end up losing out, regardless of the merits of their case.

## EXPLORING ALTERNATIVE TAX SYSTEMS

Given the extraordinary complexity and inefficiency of the current tax code, some have argued for comprehensive changes to the entire system of collecting taxes. One approach would be to replace our income tax with a progressive consumption tax that imposes a larger burden on people who consume more—generally those with greater income.

Exempting saving from taxation could bring long-run benefits. It could encourage more saving and investment, which could boost economic growth. That would be quite different from our current system, which rewards consuming today at the expense of saving for tomorrow.

A progressive consumption tax could be designed in a variety of ways, but in my opinion, a successful reform would have to accomplish three major goals: boost economic growth by raising saving, generate more revenue, and distribute tax burdens across families so that higher-consuming households paid a disproportionately higher tax.

However, a progressive consumption tax would be politically difficult to enact. There would also be challenges during the transition from the current system to the new one, which could lead policymakers to enact complicated transition rules. Without transition rules, people would be taxed when they consumed any portion of their savings—even if that savings had been built up using income that had previously been taxed under the old system.

Unfortunately, those transition rules could undermine some of the benefits of moving toward a consumption tax in the first place. Because of these considerations, a progressive consumption tax is probably a very difficult option to enact at the current time. Instead, policymakers should focus on improving our current income tax system by eliminating tax expenditures and lowering marginal tax rates, which would spur economic growth and raise revenue.

Another idea, which could help begin to address our long-term fiscal and environmental challenges simultaneously, would be to institute a carbon tax, or use a carbon tax to replace some of our other taxes. A tax on carbon would better align private incentives with the environmental costs borne by society. It would encourage more efficient use of carbon-based energy, and hasten investment in—and development of—clean-fuel technologies. While a carbon tax would raise revenue, some of that revenue could be used to lower other taxes and ensure that low-income Americans, who spend a relatively large share of their income on fuel and energy costs, aren't disproportionately affected. For all of these reasons, leading economists from across the political spectrum support carbon tax proposals, including Gregory Mankiw on the right and Joseph Stiglitz on the left.

## TAKING ACTION
## BEFORE IT'S TOO LATE

These are a number of credible, viable options for generating more revenue. Some are quite promising. None is perfect. A gradual phase in of any major reform will probably be necessary, given current economic and political conditions. All of them, ultimately, will require some compromise and sacrifice and should be paired with spending reforms in a comprehensive fiscal plan that stabilizes the debt. Every American—especially those of us who have done so well in recent years—should be prepared to contribute more to ensure that our nation will be able to avert a collision with long-term debt.

# NOT JUST AN ECONOMIC OR A FISCAL CRISIS, BUT A POLITICAL, CULTURAL, AND MORAL CRISIS

This book opened with the true story of a seemingly unsinkable ship whose captain and crew ignored explicit warnings about danger over the horizon, only to meet with a catastrophe—a tragedy—that was completely avoidable.

This was no idle analogy. Given the scale of America's mounting long-term debt challenge, and the relatively straightforward options for avoiding a collision with our long-term debt, we as citizens must insist that our leaders in Washington answer two questions: When and how are we going to change course?

Listening to all of the current partisan rancor in our nation's capital, it's easy to get discouraged about the prospects for reaching the compromises we need to solve our long-term debt challenge. The 2013 government shutdown was extremely frustrating, not to mention damaging to the trust, collaboration, and compromise that our nation needs from its political leaders.

This hyperpartisanship in Congress is a prime example of the dysfunction and extremism in our political system. It has led to politicians who preach to the extremes, not to the vital center. It has increased polarization in Congress and inhibited the basic process of bipartisan negotiation and compromise. And it has already hurt our economy. A recent study by the economic consulting firm Macroeconomic Advisers funded by the Peterson Foundation found that the uncertainty caused by U.S. lurching from fiscal crisis to fiscal crisis raised the unemployment rate in 2013 by 0.6 percentage point, equivalent to nine hundred thousand lost jobs.

But we can't lay all the blame at our political leaders' feet. Unfortunately, Americans have been sending elected leaders mixed—even contradictory—messages. On one hand, Americans say they worry about long-term debt and want Washington to bring America's debt back under control. For example, recent polling from our foundation found that 96 percent of Democrats and 97 percent of Republicans would like to see both parties work together to solve the country's long-term fiscal and economic problems. On the other hand, when the conversation turns to specific sacrifices necessary to solve our long-term fiscal challenges, the public is far less willing to accept the changes that will be required. Although the public seems willing to tolerate very modest increases in taxes and very small reductions in Social Security benefits, more significant tax increases or benefit reductions receive much less support in public opinion polls.

To some extent, this reflects a cultural shift. I mentioned at the start of this book that my parents were immigrants who came to this country with little more than a desire to live the American Dream and to provide their children access to the proverbial best education money could buy. That focus on the future was the guiding principle behind everything they did. But what are our guiding principles today? Yes, we love our children and want the best for them. But are we, as individuals and as a society, saving for their future? Too often, our culture chooses consumption and borrowing for today over saving and investing for tomorrow. We seem to take a short-term "buy now and pay later" view of everything from personal expenditures to government benefits.

Politicians do deserve blame for too often taking the easy road rather than presenting us with the hard and necessary choices. It's a practice both political parties have mastered. Many Democrats have bent over backward to convince Americans that government entitlement benefits should be permanently inviolable. At the same time, many Republicans have evolved into inflexible antitax zealots who consistently tell Americans that taxes should be lower.

But no one should feel secure on our current, unsustainable budget path. A fiscal and market crisis—or a slow-growth economic crisis—could ultimately end in unthinkable cuts to the key investments in our future and vital programs that so many vulnerable people depend on. In the end, maintaining the status quo is not in the best interest of the vulnerable. The longer we delay an agreement on a comprehensive set of reforms, the more likely the cuts will occur in the midst of a crisis, be sudden and brutal, and inflict the most pain on those who are least able to bear it.

Making changes to spending or revenues is so difficult because too many line items in the federal budget reflect the influence of powerful and effective special interest lobbies that also make large financial contributions to political leaders. Opensecrets.org shows that in 2013 there were more than twelve thousand active lobbyists who spent $3.2 billion trying to influence public policy—often seeking a special perk or tax break or subsidy inserted into the law. The revolving door between Capitol Hill and K Street (historically the home of many D.C. lobbying firms) is still whirling, and many members and senior congressional staffers eventually become lobbyists after they leave the Hill. Judging by the complexity of our tax code, to say nothing of the multitude of federal spending programs, those lobbyists have been highly successful. In fact, a study published in the *American Journal of Political Science* found that each additional dollar spent on lobbying produced an average of $6 to $20 in benefits.* We obviously need reform of our system of political contributions and our system of campaign financing in order to improve the functioning of government.

Few Americans are not connected to some lobbying group— from big banks to big telecoms; from corn and ethanol producers to peanut and sugar growers; from the federal civil service

---

*Brian Richter, Krislert Samphantharak, and Jeffrey Timmons, "Lobbying and Taxes," *American Journal of Political Science* 53, no. 4 (October 2009): 893–909.

to state and local public workers and retirees; from big pharma and health insurers and hospitals to defense and security contractors; from home builders to Realtors. At some point, you have to wonder: Who's paying full freight? And if some are, shouldn't that group feel aggrieved?

To take but one example of a powerful special interest group, consider the enormous effect of the AARP (formerly the American Association of Retired Persons) and its thirty-seven million members who regularly remind us in television commercials that if Social Security or Medicare benefits are cut, our politicians will hear from them on election day. Actually, many proposed reforms wouldn't affect those currently in or approaching retirement, yet those advertisements continue to air.

Similarly, some organizations on the right have also stymied efforts to reduce deficits. For example, Grover Norquist's Americans for Tax Reform vigorously fights against any tax increase under any circumstance and actively works to defeat members of Congress who do not accept its rigid ideology.

Of course, one of the reasons the organized lobbies are so successful is that many ordinary Americans benefit from current fiscal policies—some through direct spending and others through the tax code. Nearly half of all Americans today directly receive benefits from one or more federal programs, and forty-six million individual taxpayers take advantage of some type of tax deduction.

While comprehensive, fair, and compassionate plans to stabilize our long-term debt are needed, it is clear that we also need political counterforces to offset the power of the special interest lobbies. In a sense, we need a special interest of the general interest, or a special interest of the future. Perhaps we need a robust American Association of Young Persons (AAYP). It's the future of young people, after all, that we are mortgaging. A multimillion-member grassroots organization contacting their representatives in Congress, along with a few hundred thousand young people and their parents marching on Washington, armed with the moral force of their argument, could have an enormous effect in facilitating a comprehensive package of fiscal reforms.

Our foundation is at work trying to encourage the development of this sort of youth-oriented coalition. At the Clinton Global Initiative University, an annual meeting for more than a thousand college students from three hundred universities and seventy-five countries hosted by President Clinton, I was extraordinarily impressed by the enthusiasm, energy, and smarts of these college leaders gathered to find solutions to pressing societal challenges. We are working with the Clinton Global Initiative University on a project we are funding called Up to Us, which is a competition that energizes college students to get active on their campuses, explaining to their fellow students the fiscal and economic challenges America faces, and what they can do to help solve them. This is just an early step in what I hope will become a much broader national coalition.

In this connection, I am reminded of the old joke in which the professor asks the class: "Which is worse? Ignorance or apathy?" A sleepy student from the back of the class mutters: "I don't know and I don't care." The young must become far more aware of their projected future and far more active in doing something about it.

Ultimately, however, this is also a cause older generations of parents and grandparents must take up. As the beneficiaries of the American Dream, and of the sacrifices and hard work of earlier generations, we have a moral imperative to do what it takes to leave a stronger, more competitive economy and a more vibrant and compassionate society to our children. Consider the views of Thomas Jefferson, who wrote, "It is incumbent on every generation to pay its own debts as it goes."

It will also take inspired congressional leadership to convince Americans that keeping our long-term debt at sustainable levels will require contributions from everyone except the poor. We need leaders who can present a positive vision of a stronger economy and, at the same time, explain the negative consequences of failing to act—and soon.

We also need strong presidential leadership in both convincing the American people of the necessity to act and bringing negotiators to the table. It is certainly no easy task, but many presidents have shown what has been possible with inspired leadership. President Roosevelt did everything he could to end the Great Depression. President Eisenhower stitched our country together with his vision of the interstate highway system. President Kennedy's vision sent us to the moon. President Lyndon Johnson led the country in implementing historic civil rights legislation.

The business community must also become much more vocal about the need for long-term fiscal sustainability. There is perhaps no other group of leaders in America who understand as deeply as business leaders the effect of U.S. fiscal strength on economic growth and competitiveness, financial markets, and the success of their own businesses—as well as the cost of inaction. But until recently, business leaders were largely absent from the debate. *New York Times* columnist Thomas Friedman once called the business community MIA, or missing in action, on this fiscal issue. But here too I see encouraging signs. Budget reform champions Erskine Bowles and Alan Simpson have pulled together a coalition of CEOs (more than one hundred to date), as well as other top leaders, to help educate the public about the need to find a solution to our long-term fiscal problems.

My personal focus and that of the Peterson Foundation is to do everything possible to help create the conditions for such bipartisan cooperation and agreement so that we might reach a comprehensive agreement on sustainable fiscal policies. Toward this end, our foundation annually hosts a Fiscal Summit in Washington, D.C., that brings together leaders from Congress and the administration, from think tanks and academia, and from the media to explore paths toward reaching a bipartisan solution, and to show that a growing number of people really are concerned about the long-term debt. Since its debut in 2010, our Fiscal Summit has become the premier annual gathering on these issues, and has included conversations and interviews with President Bill Clinton, Bill Gates, Speaker John Boehner, Treasury Secretary Tim Geithner, Fed Chairman Alan Greenspan, Fed Chairman Paul Volcker, Representative Paul Ryan, and other influential policymakers and thought leaders.

The alternative to acting with foresight, timeliness, and courage is waiting for a fiscal crisis to force us to take action. If policymakers continue to engage in fiscal debacles like the fiscal cliff and paralyzing debt-limit showdowns, we may indeed hasten the day when markets lose confidence and a crisis is forced upon us. Spiking interest rates would have very damaging effects on every facet of our economy, from government programs to big and small businesses to homeowners and consumers. They could also generate unbearably high interest costs on our debt that could crowd out the investments in education, R&D, and infrastructure we will need to be successful in a more competitive world economy. As I have said, if a crisis does come, we could have to make sudden policy changes, and all the options would be far worse, with the most vulnerable Americans likely to suffer the harshest effects. How much better would it be to make timely, smart, fair, and compassionate changes to protect the vulnerable and secure our economic future?

## A LESSON FROM THE PAST AND A VISION FOR THE FUTURE

World War II was the last time that a large segment of the U.S. population made sacrifices and were very willing, if not eager, to do so. We knew the urgent goal was a peaceful and secure world, and the alternative was unthinkable. We felt we were all in it together, including those of us at home planting victory gardens, buying savings bonds, and living with rationed meat and gasoline. And in the postwar era, the Greatest Generation grew the economy and reduced federal public debt from 106 percent of

GDP in 1946 to about 25 percent of GDP over the course of the next thirty years, while at the same time launching and paying for the GI Bill, GI loans, the Marshall Plan, a massive interstate highway construction program, the space program, and the moon landing. These big goals required big visions and big resources that we are not likely to have on shoestring budgets.

I realize that today is a very different era, and fiscal struggles don't strike most people as having the same urgent, life-or-death consequences as World War II. But long-term debt does matter enormously to our nation's and our children's future. I fear that a society that can't afford big dreams will, unfortunately, have to learn to settle for low-risk, incremental advancements. The experience of World War II and the postwar years illustrates what can be done when Americans are united by grand, positive goals for our country.

The American people would be more willing to take the steps needed to build a new America if they had a positive vision of what could be accomplished by stabilizing our debt, slowing the growth of interest costs, and freeing up resources to invest in our future.

I see a bright future. I see an America that has the best educated—and most highly skilled—workforce in the world and whose workers have strong training in math, science, and technological skills. I see an innovative America that produces the best goods and services, with world-class infrastructure and high rates of saving and investment. I see an America that provides strong growth of middle-class wages and incomes. I see an America with much less inequality of income and much more upward mobility—and a country where low-income children have the same opportunities to get educated and succeed as those from higher-income families. I see an America with a modernized defense strategy that meets our current—and tomorrow's—threats at lower costs. I see an America whose safety net is secure for the vulnerable and whose entitlement programs are sustainable for the long run. I see an America with a healthcare system that provides better care at lower costs. All of these things are possible if we act to stabilize America's long-term debt. None will be achievable if we don't.

In fact, the simple truth is that we won't have a growing economy in the long run unless we stabilize our long-term debt and then bring it down. Stabilizing our long-term debt at today's level of 74 percent of GDP would be a step in the right direction, but we should go further in the decades ahead. Europe sets a maximum debt target of 60 percent of GDP, but I think America should be more ambitious and bring our long-term debt back down gradually to its historical share of GDP, which has been about 40 percent of GDP over the past forty years.

Changing our current course will require tough decisions by the American people. To build support for those decisions, our leaders must be clear about what we gain tomorrow for what we give up today.

The America I envision for the future is one of truly shared opportunity, but also shared responsibility. I want an America that is a leading force for peace and prosperity in a much more competitive and integrated world. I want an America that does more saving and investing and less borrowing. I want an America that is energy independent, with a strong foundation of innovation. I want an America that provides its children with a level of education that empowers them to improve their standard of living in a far more knowledge-based and competitive global economy, rather than leaving them unprepared, burdened with debt, and robbed of the opportunities that should be their birthright. I want an America that cares for the poor and vulnerable while also making tough choices to ensure that we have the resources to compete in a more globalized world economy.

These may be dreams, but like the best dreams they are both worthwhile and achievable. They are rooted in the shared experiences that my generation saw and lived through. As I indicated earlier, I started my life as the son of poor Greek immigrants scratching out a living in the heartland of America. It's the American way of life that made it possible for my brother and me to build on our parents' sacrifices. It's a way of life that isn't lost, but has been diminished by a combination of circumstances that we can change through collaboration, hard work, and sacrifice. We must, again in the words of former president Bill Clinton, "get America back in the future business."

At the end of the day, I believe we'll get this right. Over the last two centuries, our country has encountered many serious challenges, but we've always managed to overcome them and keep moving forward. We benefit from a remarkable endowment of resources, from our innovative entrepreneurs to the vast energy sources recently unlocked by new technology. I believe that we can once again tap into the spirit that made America great, and ensure that the United States we build for the future is dynamic, innovative, competitive, compassionate, and full of opportunity to bring back the American Dream.

# ACKNOWLEDGMENTS

I relied on the work of many others in writing this book, but I want to acknowledge a few in particular for their significant contributions:

First, I want to thank Doug Hamilton and Ed Walsh for their untold hours of dedicated assistance. They were a source of valuable counsel, helping to shape the book's direction and themes. I am also grateful for the hard work of Doug's talented colleagues in the foundation's research department who provided the many facts, figures, charts, and statistical insights that help elucidate the nature of our fiscal challenge.

Second, as I've said on many occasions, I've had a life full of dumb luck. A prime example of that good fortune is the fact that I have a son who not only is, by unanimous consent of all who work with him, truly brilliant but who also shares my passion for fiscal issues. I thank Michael for his efforts on this book as well as at our foundation, where he serves as president and COO and makes his father both happy and proud.

# APPENDIX I

Charts

## MANDATORY SPENDING ACCOUNTS FOR ALMOST 60 PERCENT OF THE BUDGET

### 2013 Total Spending: $3,455 Billion

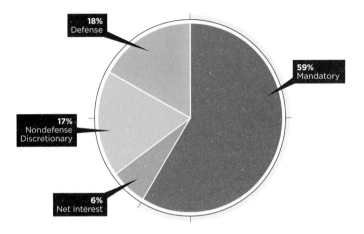

18%
Defense

59%
Mandatory

17%
Nondefense
Discretionary

6%
Net Interest

SOURCE: Office of Management and Budget, *Budget of the United States Government, Fiscal Year 2015*, March 2014. Compiled by PGPF.
NOTE: Mandatory spending includes major entitlement programs such as Social Security, Medicare, and Medicaid.

## INDIVIDUAL INCOME AND PAYROLL TAXES COMPRISE MOST OF FEDERAL RECEIPTS

### 2013 Total Revenues: $2,774 Billion

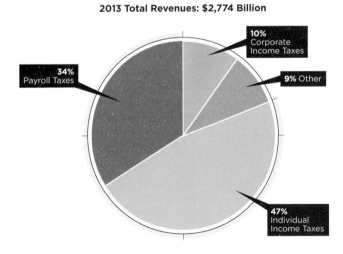

10%
Corporate
Income Taxes

9% Other

34%
Payroll Taxes

47%
Individual
Income Taxes

SOURCE: Congressional Budget Office, *The Budget and Economic Outlook: 2014 to 2024*, February 2014. Compiled by PGPF.
NOTE: "Other" includes excise taxes, customs duties, estate and gift taxes, and miscellaneous sources.

# SPENDING FOR MAJOR HEALTH PROGRAMS AND SOCIAL SECURITY WILL CONTINUE TO CLIMB RAPIDLY OVER THE LONG TERM

**Federal Spending** (Percentage of GDP)

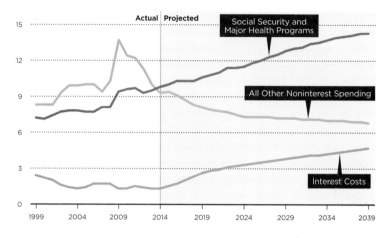

SOURCE: Congressional Budget Office, *The 2014 Long-Term Budget Outlook,* July 2014. Compiled by PGPF.
NOTE: All projections are from CBO's current-law scenario.

# FEDERAL ENTITLEMENT PROGRAMS ARE PROJECTED TO DOUBLE AS A PERCENTAGE OF GDP UNDER CURRENT LAW

**Federal Spending** (Percentage of GDP)

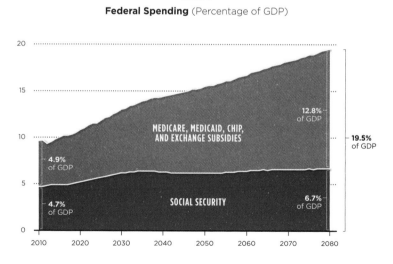

SOURCE: Congressional Budget Office, *The 2014 Long-Term Budget Outlook,* July 2014. Compiled by PGPF.
NOTE: All projections are from CBO's current-law scenario. CHIP is the Children's Health Insurance Program.
Eligibility for CHIP is based on household income and varies by state.

## MANDATORY PROGRAMS AND INTEREST COSTS WILL TAKE OVER MORE OF THE FEDERAL BUDGET, CROWDING OUT DISCRETIONARY PROGRAMS

(Percentage of federal spending)

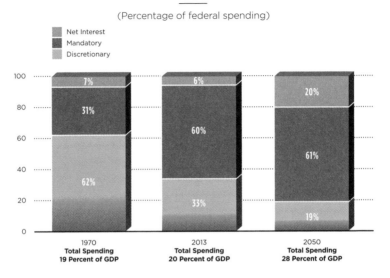

- Net Interest
- Mandatory
- Discretionary

1970
**Total Spending**
**19 Percent of GDP**

2013
**Total Spending**
**20 Percent of GDP**

2050
**Total Spending**
**28 Percent of GDP**

**SOURCE:** Congressional Budget Office, *Budget and Economic Outlook: 2014 to 2024,* February 2014, and PGPF projections based on data from the Congressional Budget Office, *The 2014 Long-Term Budget Outlook,* July 2014. Calculated by PGPF.
**NOTE:** Projections are based on CBO's current-law scenario. Numbers may not sum to totals because of rounding. Mandatory programs include Social Security, major federal health programs, other entitlement programs, and offsetting receipts.

## R&D, INFRASTRUCTURE, AND EDUCATION SPENDING ARE SMALL PARTS OF THE TOTAL FEDERAL BUDGET, BUT EACH IS VITAL FOR FUTURE ECONOMIC GROWTH

**Spending as a Percentage of Total Outlays**

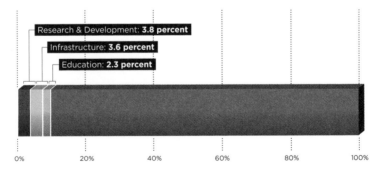

Research & Development: **3.8 percent**

Infrastructure: **3.6 percent**

Education: **2.3 percent**

**SOURCE:** Office of Management and Budget, *Budget of the United States Government, Fiscal Year 2015,* March 2014. Compiled by PGPF.
**NOTE:** Infrastructure excludes defense.

# BY 2066, PROJECTED INTEREST COSTS ON THE FEDERAL DEBT WILL EXCEED ALL FEDERAL REVENUE. IF INTEREST RATES ARE JUST TWO PERCENTAGE POINTS HIGHER, THIS WILL OCCUR TWENTY YEARS SOONER.

(Percentage of GDP)

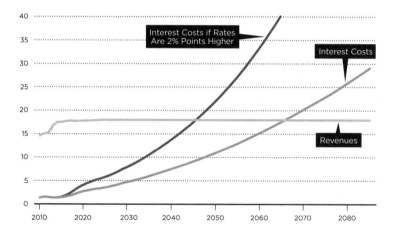

**SOURCE:** Congressional Budget Office, *An Update to the Budget and Economic Outlook: 2014 to 2024,* August 2014, and *The 2014 Long-Term Budget Outlook,* July 2014, and *How Different Future Interest Rates Would Affect Budget Deficits,* May 2013. Calculations by PGPF.
**NOTE:** Projections are based on CBO's alternative fiscal scenario. The effective interest rate on debt rises gradually until it is two percentage points higher than CBO's baseline projected rates. The projections assume revenues are held at about 18 percent of GDP in the long run, slightly higher than their historical average.

## STABILIZING OUR NATIONAL DEBT THROUGH SPENDING CUTS OR REVENUE INCREASES ALONE WOULD REQUIRE DRACONIAN POLICY CHANGES

(Percentage of GDP)

Bar chart. Left bar labeled "↓ 24%" with text: USING SPENDING DECREASES ALONE TO STABILIZE THE DEBT OVER FIFTY YEARS, WE WOULD NEED TO PERMANENTLY CUT THE BUDGET BY 24%. X-axis label: Using Spending Cuts Alone.

Right bar labeled "↑ 31%" with text: USING REVENUE INCREASES ALONE TO STABILIZE THE DEBT OVER FIFTY YEARS, WE WOULD NEED TO PERMANENTLY RAISE TAXES BY 31%. X-axis label: Using Revenue Increases Alone.

Y-axis: 0, 5, 10, 15, 20, 25.

SOURCE: Congressional Budget Office, *Updated Budget Projections: 2014 to 2024,* April 2014, and *The 2014 Long-Term Budget Outlook,* July 2014. Calculations by PGPF.
NOTE: Spending refers to noninterest spending. The spending cuts or revenue increases are the amounts needed to close the fifty-year fiscal gap and put debt on a sustainable path. The projections are based on CBO's alternative fiscal scenario.

# SOLUTIONS DO EXIST: PGPF SOLUTIONS INITIATIVE PLANS FROM FIVE THINK TANKS SHOW DECLINING FEDERAL DEBT THROUGH 2037

**Debt Held by the Public** (Percentage of GDP)

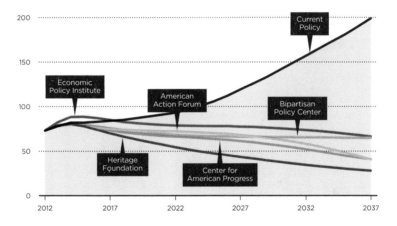

SOURCE: Peter G. Peterson Foundation, *Solutions Initiative II*, November 2012.
See pgpf.org/fiscalcliff/solutionsinitiative for more details.

# THE U.S. TAX SYSTEM IS PROGRESSIVE, WITH HIGHER-INCOME TAXPAYERS FACING HIGHER TAX RATES

**Average Tax Rate** (Percentage of cash income)

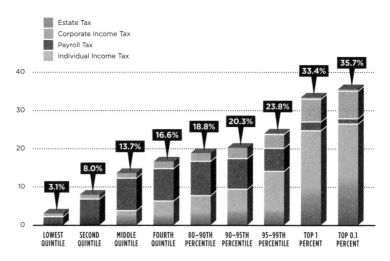

SOURCE: Tax Policy Center, *Baseline Average Effective Federal Tax Rates by Cash Income Percentile 2014,* July 2013. Data are for 2014. Compiled by PGPF.
NOTE: Individual income tax rates for the lowest and second lowest quintiles are negative and are netted against the payroll tax rate. A quintile is one fifth of the population. Calculations assume that employees also pay the employer portion of payroll taxes in the form of reduced wages. In 2013 dollars, the cash income breaks are 20%: $24,191; 40%: $47,261; 60%: $79,521; 80%: $134,266; 90%: $180,482; 95%: $261,471; 99%: $615,048; 99.9%: $3,170,865.

# GENERAL REVENUE—NOT THE MEDICARE PAYROLL TAX—IS NOW THE LARGEST SOURCE OF MEDICARE'S FINANCING

**Percentage of Total Medicare Income**

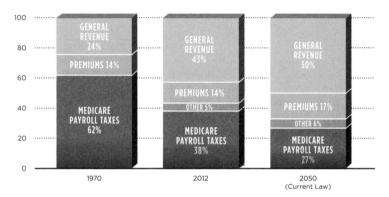

**SOURCE:** Centers for Medicare and Medicaid Services, *The 2014 Annual Report of the Boards of Trustees of the Federal Hospital Insurance and Federal Supplementary Medical Insurance Trust Funds,* July 2014. Compiled by PGPF.
**NOTE:** "Other" includes proceeds from the taxation of Social Security benefits, which help to finance Medicare hospital insurance costs as well as drug fees and state transfers. General revenues are resources that come from the general fund of the Treasury.

# THE ELDERLY POPULATION IS GROWING RAPIDLY AND LIVING LONGER

**Population** (Millions)

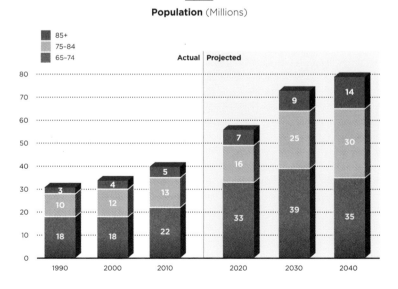

**SOURCE:** U.S. Census Bureau, *Historical National Intercensal Estimates* and *2012 National Population Projections.* Compiled by PGPF.

## MEDICAID PROVIDES HEALTH INSURANCE TO LOW-INCOME AMERICANS. CHILDREN MAKE UP NEARLY HALF OF THE PROGRAM'S ENROLLMENT, BUT MOST SPENDING IS DIRECTED TOWARD THE ELDERLY AND DISABLED.

### Percentage of Total Medicaid Program

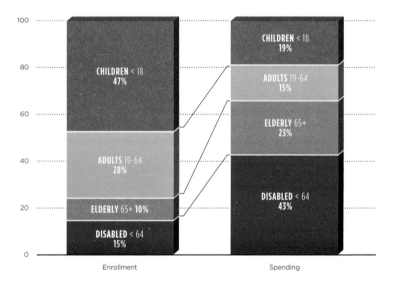

SOURCE: Medicaid and CHIP Payment and Access Commission, *MACStats,* June 2014. Compiled by PGPF.
NOTE: Data are from FY 2011.

# MORE THAN ONE THIRD OF AMERICAN CHILDREN ARE COVERED BY MEDICAID OR THE CHILDREN'S HEALTH INSURANCE PROGRAM (CHIP)

### Percentage of American Children

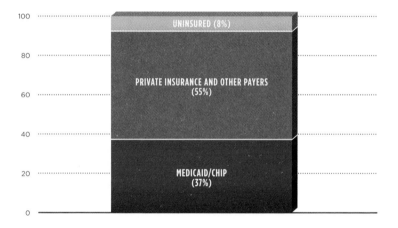

SOURCE: Medicaid and CHIP Payment and Access Commission, March 2014 MACStats. Compiled by PGPF.
NOTE: Data are from 2013. "Other payers" includes military health plans, Medicare's coverage of children, and other government programs.

# MEDICARE SPENDING PER BENEFICIARY VARIES DRAMATICALLY ACROSS REGIONS, EVEN AFTER ADJUSTING FOR ECONOMIC AND DEMOGRAPHIC DIFFERENCES

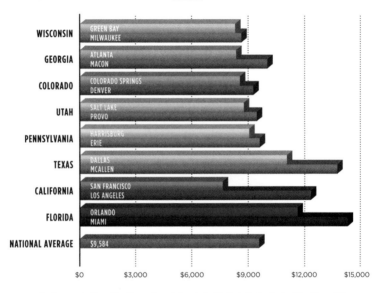

**SOURCE:** The Dartmouth Atlas of Healthcare, *Care of Chronically Ill Patients During the Last Two Years of Life.*
Compiled by PGPF.
**NOTE:** Spending figures are for 2010. Figures are adjusted for race, sex, age, and regional price differences.

# U.S. EDUCATION SPENDING IS RELATIVELY HIGH, YET OUR STUDENTS DO NOT RANK HIGHLY ON INTERNATIONAL COMPARISONS OF MATH SKILLS

| | PER PUPIL SPENDING | MATH SCORE RANK |
|---|---|---|
| Korea | $8,122 | 1 |
| Japan | $8,502 | 2 |
| Switzerland | $13,411 | 3 |
| Netherlands | $10,030 | 4 |
| Estonia | $6,149 | 5 |
| United States | $11,831 | 27 |
| **OECD Average** | **$8,617** | — |

SOURCE: National Center for Education Statistics, *PISA 2012 Results, 2013,* and the Organization for Economic Cooperation and Development, *Factbook 2013,* January 2013. Compiled by PGPF.
NOTE: Spending per student is in 2009 U.S. dollars adjusted for purchasing power parity (PPP). Rank compares the country's average student score for mathematics on the PISA test with that of other OECD countries.

# MANY AMERICANS BORN IN THE TOP AND BOTTOM INCOME QUINTILES REMAIN IN THOSE INCOME GROUPS AS ADULTS

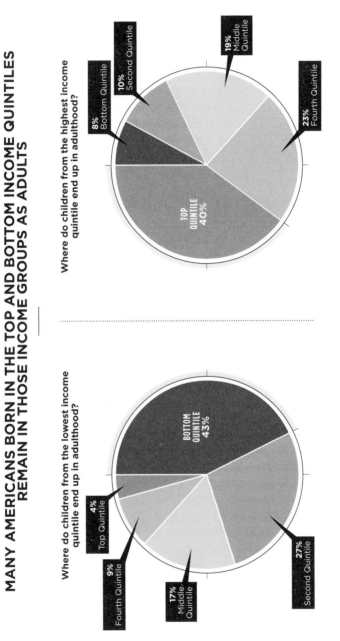

**Where do children from the lowest income quintile end up in adulthood?**

- **4%** Top Quintile
- **9%** Fourth Quintile
- **17%** Middle Quintile
- **27%** Second Quintile
- **BOTTOM QUINTILE 43%**

**Where do children from the highest income quintile end up in adulthood?**

- **8%** Bottom Quintile
- **10%** Second Quintile
- **19%** Middle Quintile
- **23%** Fourth Quintile
- **TOP QUINTILE 40%**

**SOURCE:** The Pew Charitable Trusts, *Pursuing the American Dream: Economic Mobility Across Generations*, July 2012. Compiled by PGPF.
**NOTE:** Family-level income data are from 2009 and are adjusted for family size.

# THOUGH OFTEN OVERLOOKED, STATE AND LOCAL DEBT ADDS CONSIDERABLY TO OUR NATION'S FISCAL CHALLENGES

**Debt Outstanding** (Percentage of GDP)

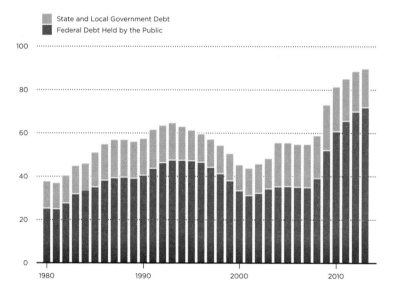

**SOURCE:** Board of Governors of the Federal Reserve System, *Financial Accounts of the United States,* March 2014, and the Congressional Budget Office, *The Budget and Economic Outlook: 2014 to 2024,* February 2014. Compiled by PGPF.

# COMPARED WITH OTHER ADVANCED COUNTRIES, THE UNITED STATES HAS HAD A LOW NATIONAL SAVING RATE

**Net National Saving Rate** (Percentage of GDP)

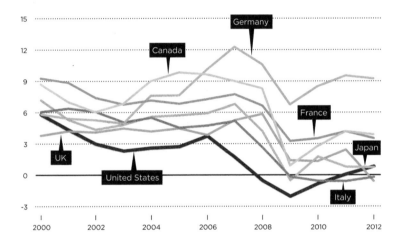

**SOURCE:** Organization for Economic Cooperation and Development, *National Accounts at a Glance*, April 2014. Compiled by PGPF.

# APPENDIX II

# A Note on Budget Projections

The CBO's long-term projections have received a great deal of attention in the media. Under its so-called current-law projection, the CBO shows that federal debt will rise to 106 percent of GDP within twenty-five years. At that level, debt would be higher than it has been at any point in U.S. history except for one year around World War II. It would be much higher than the 35 percent of GDP that it was in 2007—and the 24 percent of GDP that it has averaged since 1790. The CBO warns that high and rising levels of debt would harm our economy.

However, as disquieting as those projections are, I believe they seriously understate the true magnitude of the long-term fiscal challenges facing the United States because they are based on a number of optimistic assumptions about future budget policy. For example, they assume that discretionary spending will be sharply constrained, unpopular sequesters will remain in place, physician reimbursement rates under Medicare will drop dramatically, popular tax breaks will be allowed to expire, and revenues will rise well above historical averages.

If lawmakers fail to stay on this assumed path of fiscal restraint, federal debt will soar sharply above 100 percent of GDP. For example, the CBO shows that under an alternative fiscal scenario that makes less optimistic assumptions and incorporates the negative effects of debt on the economy, federal debt would skyrocket to 183 percent of GDP within twenty-five years.

The assumptions about discretionary spending in the current-law projections are especially implausible. These discretionary programs are an important part of the budget and cover a wide range of government activities including defense, scientific research, infrastructure, and education, as well as law enforcement, national parks, NASA, food safety inspections, federal pay, and grants to state and local governments.

In its current-law projections, the CBO assumes that spending on those programs will decline significantly from 7.2 percent of GDP in 2013 to 5.2 percent of GDP in 2025 and then remain at that low level thereafter. Although current law imposes tight caps on discretionary spending through 2021, it seems very doubtful that lawmakers would adhere to such tight restraints indefinitely. At 5.2 percent of GDP, discretionary spending would be well below its average of 7.3 percent of GDP over the past twenty years—and below the *lowest* point it has been in the past fifty years, which was 6.0 percent of GDP in 1999.

# DISCRETIONARY SPENDING FUNDS A
# WIDE RANGE OF GOVERNMENT PROGRAMS

**Discretionary Spending: 35% of Total Federal Spending**

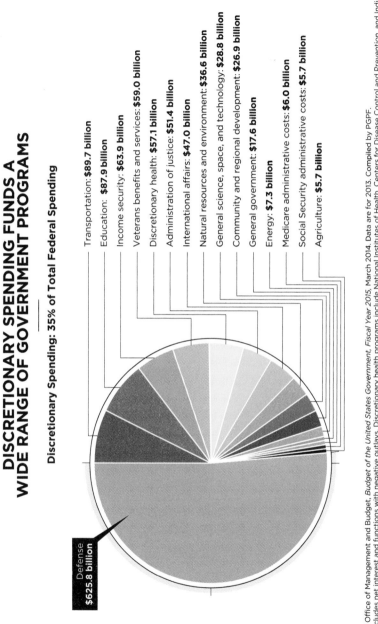

Transportation: **$89.7 billion**

Education: **$87.9 billion**

Income security: **$63.9 billion**

Veterans benefits and services: **$59.0 billion**

Discretionary health: **$57.1 billion**

Administration of justice: **$51.4 billion**

International affairs: **$47.0 billion**

Natural resources and environment: **$36.6 billion**

General science, space, and technology: **$28.8 billion**

Community and regional development: **$26.9 billion**

General government: **$17.6 billion**

Energy: **$7.3 billion**

Medicare administrative costs: **$6.0 billion**

Social Security administrative costs: **$5.7 billion**

Agriculture: **$5.7 billion**

Defense
**$625.8 billion**

**SOURCE:** Office of Management and Budget, *Budget of the United States Government, Fiscal Year 2015*, March 2014. Data are for 2013. Compiled by PGPF.
**NOTE:** Excludes net interest and functions with negative outlays. Discretionary health programs include National Institutes of Health, Centers for Disease Control and Prevention, and Indian Health Service.

## DISCRETIONARY SPENDING IS PROJECTED TO DECLINE BELOW ITS HISTORICAL SHARE OF GDP

**Discretionary Spending** (Percentage of GDP)

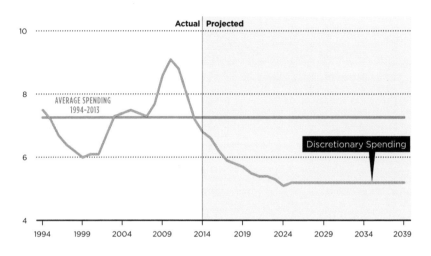

SOURCE: Congressional Budget Office, *The 2014 Long-Term Budget Outlook*, July 2014, and *Historical Budget Data*, April 2014. Compiled by PGPF.
NOTE: Projections are from CBO's current-law scenario.

Indeed, Congress has already had great difficulty bringing discretionary spending under the budget caps for 2014. If lawmakers had trouble reducing discretionary spending in 2014 when it was 6.8 percent of GDP, is it plausible to expect that discretionary spending will be reduced to 5.2 percent of GDP in coming years?

And if lawmakers actually achieved that target, would it be a wise and sensible choice for the nation? Discretionary spending funds many programs that could help our economy grow, such as infrastructure, R&D, skills training, and education.

How will our nation be able to succeed in a vastly more competitive and technological global economy if discretionary programs are constrained so tightly?

The current-law projections also embody a number of other optimistic assumptions about future budget policy. They assume that Medicare's reimbursement rates for physicians will drop by about 24 percent on April 1, 2015 as required by current law, even though policymakers have overridden those reductions many times in the past.

On the revenue side of the budget, the current-law projections assume that a large number of tax provisions will expire in coming years as scheduled under current law. In the past, lawmakers have routinely extended those provisions, yet the CBO's current-law projections assume that all of those tax provisions will expire permanently. These provisions include the tax credit for research and experimentation.

Finally, the CBO's current-law projections assume that lawmakers will not change the tax code even as more and more taxpayers are pushed into higher tax brackets as their real incomes rise. This will have significant—and unintended—consequences on many middle-class and poor households. For example, under current law, the CBO estimates that the fraction of Social Security benefits subject to tax will climb from 30 percent to 50 percent over the next twenty-five years, and the value of the personal exemption relative to income will fall by more than 30 percent. As the CBO notes in *The 2014 Long-Term Budget Outlook:* "If no changes in tax law were enacted in the future, the effects of the tax system in 2039 would differ in significant ways from what those effects are today. Average taxpayers *at all income levels* [emphasis added] would pay a greater share of income in taxes than similar taxpayers do now." Although all taxpayers would face a higher tax burden under continuation of current law, low-income taxpayers would be significantly affected. For example, the effective income and payroll tax rate paid by single taxpayers with half the median income would climb by 38 percent over the next twenty-five years under current law, according to the CBO.

Because many of the assumptions beneath the current projections can be questioned, the CBO also prepared an alternative fiscal scenario. In that scenario, discretionary spending gradually rises back up to its historical average in the long run; the sequester is repealed; Medicare's scheduled reduction in physician reimbursement rates is overridden; expiring tax provisions are permanently extended; and revenues remain at 18.0 percent of GDP in 2024 instead of rising to 19.4 percent of GDP in 2039 (and to 23.9 percent of GDP in 2089) as they would under current law. The CBO also incorporates the feedback effects of rising debt on the economy in some of its projections. As debt rises, it crowds out capital investment, reduces productivity, and slows the growth of wages and incomes. Higher debt also puts upward pressure on interest rates in the CBO's alternative projections, causing interest costs to climb, which accelerate the growth of debt.

Under the alternative fiscal scenario, the CBO estimates that federal debt would climb to 183 percent of GDP within twenty-five years. At these levels, debt would be in territory that would be very hazardous to economic growth.

# INDEX

| Page numbers in *italics* refer to illustrations. |